AN EVOLUTIONARY LEAP

AN EVOLUTIONARY LEAP
Colin Wilson on Psychology

Colin Stanley

KARNAC

First published in 2016 by
Karnac Books Ltd
118 Finchley Road
London NW3 5HT

British Library Cataloguing in Publication Data

A C.I.P. for this book is available from the British Library

ISBN-13: 978-1-78220-444-2

Typeset by V Publishing Solutions Pvt Ltd., Chennai, India

Printed in Great Britain

www.karnacbooks.com

For Gail

CONTENTS

ACKNOWLEDGEMENT

My thanks to George C. Poulos and Maurice Bassett.

PERMISSIONS

ABOUT THE AUTHORS

Colin Stanley was born in Topsham, Devon, UK in 1952 and educated at Exmouth School. Beginning in 1970, he worked for Devon Library Services, studying for two years in London, before moving to Bovey Tracey with his wife, Gail, and thence to Nottingham where he worked for the University of Nottingham until July 2005.

One of the founders and managing editor of Paupers' Press, he now works part-time for the Nottingham Trent University and spends the rest at the cinema and theatre, listening to music, writing, editing, reading, and watching cricket.

The author of two experimental novels, a slim volume of nonsense verse, and several books and booklets about Colin Wilson and his work, he is the editor of *Colin Wilson Studies*, a series of books and extended essays, written by Wilson scholars worldwide. His collection of Wilson's work now forms *The Colin Wilson Collection* at the University of Nottingham, an archive opened in the summer of 2011 and which now includes many of the author's manuscripts.

He now resides with Gail by the River Trent, close to Trent Bridge cricket ground, their two children, Andrew and Katrina-Jane, having long since moved on.

Colin Wilson was born in the East Midlands city of Leicester in 1931. After the phenomenal success of his first book *The Outsider* in 1956, he moved to Cornwall where he pursued a successful career as a writer, producing over 150 titles in fifty-five years. Essentially an existential philosopher, he has also written on crime, psychology, sex, the occult, literature, music, unexplained phenomena, history, pre-history, and over twenty novels in various genres. He died in December 2013.

PREFACE

Colin Wilson and Abraham Maslow

Colin Wilson's contribution to the field of psychology is much underrated and although it owes a debt to his association with Abraham Maslow (1908–1970)—in particular his concept of "peak experiences" (PEs), which assured Wilson that we *can*, and frequently *do*, rise above the "triviality of everydayness" and access a heightened form of consciousness (albeit briefly)—many of his ideas in this field had already been formulated before the one became aware of the other's work. Indeed, it was Maslow, then a professor at Brandeis University, who made the initial contact, writing to Wilson in 1963, after reading his *The Age of Defeat* (aka *The Stature of Man* in the US), published in 1959: "He explained that he had been impressed with the optimism of *The Stature of Man*, and about the way I had pinpointed the sense of defeat that permeates our culture ...", Wilson wrote in his autobiography *Dreaming to Some Purpose* (Wilson, 2003, p. 208).

Maslow had apparently come to have doubts about Freud's sexual theory. Wilson commented: "This is something I had felt strongly for years: Freud's view that all our deepest urges are sexual seemed to me to leave out some of the most important members of the human race, from Leonardo to Bernard Shaw ..." (ibid., p. 208). A correspondence struck up between them during which Maslow sent Wilson a selection of his papers:

> What fascinated me most about the Maslow material was his remark that, as a psychologist, he had got tired of studying sick people because they talked about nothing but their sickness. So he looked around for the healthiest people he could find, and studied them instead. And he quickly made an interesting discovery: all his healthy subjects had, with a fair degree of frequency, moments of sudden immense happiness. He came to call these "peak experiences" (or PEs). The peak experience was not necessarily mystical in the religious sense—just a sudden overflowing of sheer joy and vitality. (ibid., p. 209)

Clearly impressed, Wilson wrote to Maslow on 8 July 1964 enclosing an eleven-page essay on Maslow's work intended to be the conclusion to a book he was writing: *The Anatomy of Human Greatness*, a summary of his six "Outsider Cycle" books. The essay, labelled "Maslow and the peak experience", commenced: "I come now to the man who seems to me to be doing some of the most important work in the world in this field of existential psychology ..." As it happened *Anatomy ...*, as it then stood, was never published, being replaced by *Introduction to the New Existentialism* in 1966 in which Maslow is not discussed in such detail. However, when he sent a copy of the latter to him, Maslow immediately contacted Wilson's US publisher, Houghton Mifflin, and pre-ordered 100 copies for his undergraduate students! In a letter to Wilson dated 10 October 1969 he affirmed that: "... your Existential book was a major textbook job; ... *Beyond the Outsider* was both fascinating and important philosophical reading; and ... I enjoyed your autobiography very much and think that in it you have advanced your major ideas toward greater maturity, lucidity, clarity" (The "autobiography" that Maslow mentions was *Voyage to a Beginning* (Wilson's "preliminary autobiography") (London: Cecil & Amelia Woolf, 1969. Extended version: New York: Crown Publishers, 1969)).

The two first met on 1 November 1966 when Wilson took time off from his position as writer-in-residence at Hollins College, Virginia, to visit Maslow at Brandeis University:

I had seen photographs of Abe, with his small grey moustache and hair combed straight back, so it looked almost like a crew cut. ... Photographs gave no impression of his main characteristic—his immense warmth and kindness. He was one of the few people I have met who struck me as genuinely *good*. (ibid., p. 260)

Regular readers of Wilson's books will know that he valued his fiction as much, if not more, than his non-fiction work, and used his novels to put his ideas into action. Unsurprisingly then, Maslow was written into his 1969 novel *The Philosopher's Stone* and the later *The Black Room* (1971). In a letter to Maslow dated 15 September 1968 he wrote:

I finished a novel—one of my best, I think—a sequel to *The Mind Parasites*, in which I manage to write about super-normal states of consciousness with far more precision than I achieved in the other book. You figure very largely in the first part, again under the name of Aaron Marks, and I call your PEs "value experiences", and describe a series of experiments Marks does to cure alcoholics with the use of VEs, and then lengthening human life by giving intelligent old people VEs. I'll try and let you have a typescript of the book soon, but I'm going to dedicate it to you, if that's ok ...[1]

Clearly Maslow was not keen on a book being dedicated to him; when *The Philosopher's Stone* appeared in print the dedicatee was "Jorge Luis Borges". Wilson's remark about Maslow figuring *again* as Aaron Marks refers to a short story, "Margin of Darkness", eventually incorporated into *The Black Room*, which appeared in *The Minnesota Review* in 1966 (Vol. 6, pp. 268–295).

In the same letter Wilson suggested that he write a full-length book about Maslow: "... so I'm carefully collecting all the papers you've sent me, and in due course, I'll have to spend a week with you getting purely biographical material." This led to Maslow recording four audio tapes and forwarding them to Wilson which he used as a basis for his book *New Pathways in Psychology: Maslow and the Post-Freudian Revolution*, published by Victor Gollancz in 1972, two years after his subject's death (I recall, from one of my visits to Wilson, him bemoaning the fact that these tapes had been stolen from his house in Cornwall, sometime in the 1980s, by a Dutch journalist who purported to be a student of Maslow's work).

Wilson started work on the book when he was writer-in-residence at The Mediterranean Institute of Dowling College at Deya, Mallorca, Spain. In a long letter to Maslow from there on 5 November 1969, he wrote:

> I am working on the assumption that you are the single most important figure in psychology since Freud, and a real turning point. I shall speak of the others, Frankl, Rogers, Rollo May, Boss etc. But I want this account of you to have a beautiful FLOW and simplicity, *like a detective story*. It may well take its place as the foundation of all future work on you ...

It would appear from their correspondence, shortly before his sudden death on 8 June 1970, that Maslow was attempting to secure a fellowship for Wilson at an American university in order to "... bring ... you to this country for a while—not only for your sake but so that we could work together on my ideas" (letter from Maslow to Wilson dated 30 April 1970). Wilson replied enthusiastically on 7 May: "Nothing would give me greater pleasure than to work with you for a period. I'll look forward to seeing what happens ..."

It is interesting to speculate how Wilson's career may have panned out had these plans come to fruition.

Colin Stanley
Nottingham, United Kingdom

Note

1. The Wilson/Maslow correspondence is held in the Archives of the History of American Psychology at the University of Akron, Ohio.

CHAPTER ONE

The Age of Defeat (1959)

In 1957, the publisher Tom Maschler (1933-) edited a volume of essays entitled *Declaration*—a symposium containing the credos of eight so-called "Angry Young Men". In his introduction, Maschler wrote:

> We have to thank an even lower level of journalism for the phrase "Angry Young Men" which has been employed to group, without so much as an attempt at understanding, all those sharing a certain indignation against the apathy, the complacency, the idealistic bankruptcy of their environment. ... To be prejudiced against them purely because they are angry is to imagine that anger is the sole substance of their work. ... It is important to note that although most of the contributors to this volume have at some time been termed Angry Young Men they do *not* belong to a united movement. Far from it; they attack one another directly or indirectly in these pages. Some were even reluctant to appear between the same covers with others whose views they violently oppose. (Maschler, 1957, pp. 7–8)

But three contributors did, at least, have something in common: Colin Wilson, Bill Hopkins, and Stuart Holroyd. They were friends and, at that time, all rented rooms in a kind of writers' commune at a house in Chepstow Road, London (Upon leaving the premises in 1960, Hopkins commissioned his friend Laurence Bradshaw to sculpt a blue plaque which was fixed to the outside wall near the front door. It read: "In this house lived, 1955–1960, Colin Wilson, John Braine, Stuart Holroyd, Tom Greenwell, Greta Detloff, Bill Hopkins. Hallowed be these precincts." This was taken down soon afterwards and nothing is now known of its whereabouts).

The Age of Defeat (published as *The Stature of Man* in the US), the third book in Colin Wilson's "Outsider Cycle",[1] was published in the UK by Victor Gollancz in September 1959. In his new introduction to the 2001 Paupers' Press edition, Wilson writes:

> The [*Age of Defeat*] was not originally intended to be published as a separate volume, but as one-third of a kind of symposium that would feature Bill Hopkins, Stuart Holroyd and myself. This came about because the three of us were thoroughly dissatisfied with a book called *Declaration*, which had appeared in 1957, and in which the three of us had also featured. It was ... intended to be a series of "statements of belief" by a number of the so-called "Angry Young Men" ... [and] aroused a lot of hostility. (Wilson, 2001a, p. 11)

He continues:

> [The] basic theme [of this new book] would be the "vanishing hero"—that inability of modern writers to create what Bill called "monumental characters". I would treat the subject from the literary point of view, Stuart from the religious point of view, Bill from the political point of view.
>
> The problem was that Bill and Stuart were slower writers ... so I wrote my part of the ... book in the first half of 1958 and sent it to my publisher. Gollancz immediately suggested that he should publish it on its own. Bill and Stuart were obviously relieved to be let off the hook, for neither of them had even started their contributions ... (ibid., p. 14)

The book is divided into five parts sandwiched by an introduction and a postscript. The above-mentioned Paupers' Press edition adds a further introduction in which Wilson writes:

> Although I would not count *The Age of Defeat* as one of my most successful books ... it brought me ... one important contact: an American professor of psychology called Abraham Maslow. It was Maslow who, after reading the American edition ... wrote me a letter in which he told me that he had been preoccupied with the same problem for a long time. He told me how he had said to his students: "Which of you expects to be great?" And when they looked at him blankly, he said "If not you, who then?" (ibid., p. 21)

An extremely important contact for Wilson, Maslow's concept of "peak experience" (PE)—that sudden rush of pure happiness that we all experience in moments of delight—subsequently became the cornerstone of his philosophy of optimism. They remained in touch until Maslow's death in 1970 (the as-yet unpublished correspondence between the two makes for fascinating reading). His widow subsequently supplied Wilson with the tape recordings of her husband that he used as source material for the study *New Pathways in Psychology: Maslow and the Post-Freudian Revolution* (see Chapter Three).

In the original introduction subtitled "The vanishing hero", Wilson complains that most contemporary writers concern themselves with the "ordinary man" and his problems and in so doing often just deal with the most ordinary states of mind. He argues that these weak "heroes" often reflect the inadequacies of their creators and criticises James Joyce, William Faulkner, Aldous Huxley, D. H. Lawrence, and *avant-garde* writers such as Alain Robbe-Grillet:

> I decline to accept the view that the world is composed of a mass of self-deceiving fools, and a few impotently honest men who are self-divided and highly intellectual. I believe that strength and an unimpeded vital insight are possible to man. My quarrel with modern writing is based on its unconscious defeatism. (ibid., p. 21)

He reasons that heroism depends upon a sense of purpose but in a world geared towards "social thinking", where man's first duty is to society, this is extremely difficult.

Part one, therefore, concerns itself with "The evidence of sociology" and the problems that arise from increased material security: "Too much security has the effect of slackening the vital tension and weakening the urge to live" (ibid., p. 29). His thesis draws heavily on two American studies: David Riesman's *The Lonely Crowd* (1950) and William H. Whyte's *The Organization Man* (1956), which argue that Americans are becoming "other-directed" (i.e., orientated towards society) and less "inner-directed" (i.e., self-disciplined pioneers who can drive towards a goal) and increasingly "organization men" (i.e., willing to toe-the-line for a regular wage and secure job).

Wilson asserts that "... the real problem is the attitude of the individual towards himself" (ibid., p. 32). "Other-directed" people tend to divide the world into ordinary and extraordinary people, holding the extraordinary in awe but never aspiring to become one. And "... a life lived on a general level of 'insignificance'... makes for outbreaks of violence" (ibid., p. 46). "Other-directed" people, longing for the heightened intensity of "inner-direction" search for stimulation in violence. Thus the rise in sex crime (another subject that greatly interests Wilson and which he will write about at length in the future) is seen as a result of a revolt against the taboos imposed by "other-direction". Examples of sex criminals such as Peter Kürten (1883–1931), the Düsseldorf killer, are cited.

In part two, "The evidence of literature", James Jones' *From Here to Eternity* (1951), Herman Wouk's *The Caine Mutiny* (1951), and James Gould Cozzens' *By Love Possessed* (1957) are offered as examples of the "organisation man" being presented as hero even when, as in the case of *The Caine Mutiny*, it is clearly the individual who defies authority (i.e., the mutineer Maryk) that saves the day. The author, however, implies that orders should always be obeyed even if the consequences are disastrous. William Faulkner is attacked as an author who admires unheroic defeated men who somehow "endure". As for John Dos Passos: "... when society is not the hero (or villain), the hero is defeated" (ibid., p. 85). The plays of Eugene O'Neill "... are full of bewildered characters driven by their passions, and the ending is nearly always despair and defeat" (ibid., p. 85). The same can be said for Tennessee Williams. Arthur Miller "... again reveals the same preoccupation with the individual who is defeated by society, or by his own passions" (ibid., p. 86). Ernest Hemingway's "... achievement and influence are undeniable but to his younger imitators he must seem a walking declaration that defeat is unavoidable" (ibid., p. 92). And although the Beat Generation "... represent[s] a kind of revolt ... it is difficult to discover a great deal more [than] a pure reflex action against 'other-direction' ..." (ibid., pp. 92–94).

But despite a lack of "inner-directed" characters in modern English literature, Wilson believes that "... the situation in England is, on the whole, more promising than in America" (ibid., p. 104). Whereas "... the revolt of Amis, Wain and Osborne lacks direction ..." (ibid., p. 101), John Braine in *Room at the Top* (1957) and Bill Hopkins in *The Divine and the Decay* (1957) do provide "inner-directed" heroes.

In the third part, "The anatomy of insignificance", Wilson decides that "... the hero is ... a man who needs to *expand*, who needs wider fields for his activities. He is the man who cannot 'accept' the *status quo* ..." (ibid., p. 113). He then traces the history of heroes in literature from the old physical hero who "... lowered his head and charged like a bull" to the 'new' self-divided hero and posits that "... the final hero will be the man who has healed the self-division, and is again prepared to fling himself into the social struggle" (ibid., p. 120).

Romanticism "... for all its sentimentality ... never lost sight of the importance of the individual ... As soon as the reader opens a book by Hoffmann or Kleist or Brentano, he is transported into a world of greater intensity" (ibid., p. 121). But, Wilson concludes: "All that emerges from consideration of the nineteenth century is that, with occasional exceptions, its writers lost sight of the hero. Society is the true hero of most nineteenth century novels" (ibid., p. 128). An important exception, however, is Nietzsche's Zarathustra: "But his 'action' amounts only to preaching, and the world in which he preaches is an anonymous realm of fantasy ... Like Goethe's *Faust, Thus Spake Zarathustra* is an attempt to create a new hero, and an admission of failure" (ibid., p. 129).

In the early twentieth century H. G. Wells, G. K. Chesterton, and George Bernard Shaw created a temporary respite from the age of unheroic defeatism. Shaw's "Julius Caesar in *Caesar and Cleopatra* is the only serious attempt in twentieth century literature to create an undefeated hero" (ibid., p. 132). Robert Musil's hero Ulrich in *Der Mann ohne Eigenschaften* (*The Man without Qualities*) (3 vols., 1930, 1942) is given much consideration as Wilson feels "[Musil] had recreated the Faust figure in a typically modern context ... and this was a very considerable achievement ... when the unheroic premise dominated the literature of Europe and America" (ibid., p. 140).

Part four, "The fallacy of insignificance", concerns itself mainly with the existentialism of Jean-Paul Sartre (1905–1980) whose "… aim is to emphasise man's freedom and to explain the workings of that freedom" (ibid., p. 144). However, we can surrender that freedom in a number of ways, most significantly through self-deception (*mauvaise foi*):

> A man is very seldom aware of himself as a person; what he is mainly aware of … is what other people think of him … But there are certain moments in which a man knows himself as a positive reality … The result of this recognition is a knowledge of the dual nature of freedom. Man is free all the time, but he confronts his freedom only at long intervals. Between these occasions, he is free, but does not know it. To be free without knowing it is not to be free. In order to become a reality which "authenticates" existence, freedom must be grasped intuitively. (ibid., pp. 150–151)

Although Sartre "… analyses every aspect of man's uncertainty …" (ibid., p. 152) "… his limitations appear when it comes to a question of remedy" (ibid., p. 153). And "… the final index to an author's insight into 'inner-direction' is his ability to create an 'inner-directed' man, the hero. For the most part Sartre's central characters are as negative as those of any American novelist" (ibid., p. 154). Sartre is ultimately "… the dramatist of insignificance …" (ibid., p. 152).

Albert Camus (1913–1960), like Sartre,

> … has certain clearly defined limitations … [He] is interested in the position of man in the Universe … his "solution" … will be some individual vision, some reconciling insight into the condition of man … Yet … he seems to lack the temperament that can reach toward mystical insights … [and] although his final final position is one of affirmation, he makes the impression of being a negative writer … There is still a strong element of the "cult of the ordinary chap" in him. (ibid., pp. 163–164)

(The reader should be aware that Wilson is writing in 1959, one year *before* Camus' death.)

Finally, Wilson asks: "Is it possible for existentialism to become something more positive?" (ibid., p. 165). This sets the scene for the introduction of his new existentialism which is outlined in part five, "The stature of man": "I envisage the new existentialism as a mystical revolt, based upon recognition of the irrational urge that underlies man's conscious reason. [There is a] need to give life an additional dimension of purpose" (ibid., p. 189). This revolt should, according to Wilson, take place on two levels: philosophical and creative. "On the creative level, it would be a revolt against the unheroic premise, the attempt to create heroes who possess a vision that extends beyond the particularities of environment" (ibid., p. 189). "As a philosophy, existentialism must emphasise the primacy of the will, the importance of the individual, the final unpredictability and freedom of even the most 'neurotic' and conditioned human being" (ibid., p. 191).

In this book Wilson sets the benchmark for his own fiction: "The responsibility of literature in the twentieth century becomes appallingly clear: to illuminate man's freedom" (ibid., p. 200). True to his word, for the past fifty years, since the first edition of *The Age of Defeat* was published, Wilson has set about the task of systematically re-establishing the hero—from Gerard Sorme in *Ritual in the Dark* (1960), his first novel, to Niall, the indomitable hero of the epic fantasy *Spider World* (4 vols., 1987–2003)—in an attempt to show us all that we too can grasp life's "additional dimension of purpose".

* * *

Contemporary reviews of the book were not complimentary, although after the unjust condemnation of his previous work *Religion and the Rebel*, it has to be said that criticism *was* tempered somewhat. After such a pounding, Wilson could have been excused for not putting pen to paper again. But he was not to be browbeaten into abandoning his philosophical stance no matter how unpopular it was considered to be. J. Rayner Heppenstall, in a largely critical review did, however, begrudgingly admit:

> Mr. Wilson has now published a book in which he urges us to pull our socks up, to adopt a positive attitude instead of feeling downcast, to express our individualities instead of succumbing to mass pressures and, in short, to be heroes ... Few of us would deny that there is something in what [he] says ... (Heppenstall, 1959, p. 503)

John A. Weigel comments:

> The harsh responses to [Wilson's] good intentions reinforced his determination to continue his mission not only to illuminate man's

freedom in his novels but also to evaluate in his critical writings the relative success and failure of others. (Weigel, 1975, p. 50)

Clifford P. Bendau concludes:

Wilson's concept of the "existential hero" draws together his ideas concerning freedom, will and evolution. As part of his philosophy, it reflects his belief in the positive nature of reality, as well as his theoretical positions on the nature and function of imagination ... The writer, in order to utilize the true portrait of the hero, must be cognizant of the interworkings of literature, the imagination, and human values. Only then, claims Wilson, will the writer have the "strength" to work hand-in-hand with the philosopher. (Bendau, 1979, pp. 18–19)

Not surprisingly then, the next volume in Wilson's "Outsider Cycle", published in 1962, was entitled *The Strength to Dream: Literature and the Imagination*.

Note

1. The "Outsider Cycle" is as follows: *The Outsider* (1956), *Religion and the Rebel* (1957), *The Age of Defeat* (*The Stature of Man* in the US) (1959), *The Strength to Dream: Literature and the Imagination* (1962), *Origins of the Sexual Impulse* (1963), *Beyond the Outsider: The Philosophy of the Future* (1965), *Introduction to the New Existentialism* (1966).

CHAPTER TWO

Origins of the Sexual Impulse (1963)

This fifth volume in Colin Wilson's "Outsider Cycle" was published in Britain by Arthur Barker on 10 May 1963 and in the US by G. P. Putnam's Sons the following month. The book is

> ... concerned mainly with the post-Freudian revolt against a totally analytical approach, and with raising the question of whether the methods of Gestalt psychology and of Husserl's phenomenology can be applied to the psychology of sex. (Wilson, 1970a, p. 14)

In an introductory note, Wilson explains that he is planning a "new existentialism" arguing that the "old existentialism" has recently died (around 1950, he estimates): "Before the end of this volume, I shall try to explain why I consider sex to be a valid approach to a new existentialism" (ibid., p. 14). He reveals that he is simultaneously writing a book entitled *Outline of a New Existentialism*. This obviously became his *Beyond the Outsider: The Philosophy of the Future*, (the "Outsider Cycle", book 6), published in 1965, because in a contemporary interview with *The Yorkshire Post* he describes *Origins* as: "... a Siamese twin of another book, *Beyond the Outsider*, which was about my New Existentialism" (Wilson, 1963, n.k.). Howard F. Dossor explains:

> ... Wilson saw that the way forward for Existentialism lay in the application of that essential characteristic of consciousness that Husserl had called intentionality. Since imagination was a powerful form of applied intentionality, and since the most dramatic and powerful form of imagination in modern man seemed to be demonstrated in his sexuality, a treatment of sex was unavoidable. It was, in fact, so critical that it could not be contained within a single chapter of the book on the New Existentialism and thus the book of the origins of sex was necessary. (Dossor, 1990, p. 118)

Chapter One is entitled "A general discussion of sexual aberration":

> The most obvious statement about the sexual impulse is that here is a point where man and "nature" have two different aims. The aim of nature appears to be procreation. The aim of the individual is to achieve the fullest possible satisfaction in the sexual orgasm. (op. cit., p. 18)

"A perversion," says Wilson, "is usually defined as 'an unnatural act' ... but where nature has separated its own purposes from man's as widely as in the case of sex, how are we to judge what is natural?" Tolstoy felt that "... the only normal sex is sex directed specifically to producing children" (ibid., p. 19) but the objection to this is that it is "... defining abnormality in terms of the *end* rather than the means" (ibid., p. 20) and surely, Wilson argues, it is the means by which an orgasm is procured that counts when judging "abnormality".

Acknowledging that "... the sexual instinct works on a deeper level than any other human impulse" (ibid., p. 22), Wilson goes on to make three important points about human sexuality:

1. It has a definite physical component ... "The desire of the sexual parts to achieve an orgasm" (ibid., p. 24).
2. "The component that unites and directs the human sexual impulses is purely mental or imaginative" (ibid., pp. 24–25).
3. "Of all human instincts and desires, the sexual instinct is the one that most transcends man's *conscious* awareness of himself and his purpose" (ibid., p. 25).

Wilson asserts that "... the basic activity of all living organisms is the discharging of various forms of tension" (ibid., p. 30), which can lead to a temporary broadening of consciousness: "... this need for release, for heightened consciousness, is one of the most basic human strivings" (ibid., p. 31). The sexual urge is seen as the shortest and easiest route to this release of tension and heightening of consciousness. And it can be made more potent by pushing the boundaries of "normality". D. H. Lawrence's anal eroticism is seen as an example of this. Ultimately, Tolstoy's view of sexual "abnormality" is dismissed because "... he has [not] arrived at a balanced vision of the part played by sex in man's total being" (ibid., p. 36).

The philosopher Georges Gurdjieff (1866–1949), however, is considered to be the only modern philosopher "... who has made an attempt at a unifying sex theory" (ibid., p. 25). His theory is based on the idea that man has seven centres (five basic and two "higher"). The sexual centre is the highest of the basic centres and works on a finer energy than the other four. The fact that human beings have very little knowledge of their "higher" centres—except in moments of insight (or heightened consciousness)—is very relevant because "[it implies] that our normal state of consciousness is a poor, barren half-ration" (ibid., p. 39). This, for Wilson, "... makes an excellent starting point for the study of sex" (ibid., p. 39).

Chapter Two, "Promiscuity and the Casanova impulse", examines how far the obsessive pursuit of sex is unnatural. Wilson considers the life and work of Giacomo Casanova (1725–1798), Frank Harris (author of *My Life and Loves*, 1922–27) (1856–1931), Henry Miller (1891–1980), and the Russian author Mikhail Artsybasheff (1878–1927). He feels that "Don Juanism may indicate a lack of basic self-belief [and that] among men of genuine talent ... is frequently an early stage, before more serious work claims their energy" (ibid., p. 47). He concludes that:

> The impulse to promiscuity is not explained by saying that a man's sexual desires are stronger than normal, or even by explaining that some inferiority feeling drives him to "over-compensate". This only leads to the further question: What should be the "normal" desire, and how *ought* the inferiority to be compensated? The sexual part of man's being is not like a small self-governed, self-supporting

state; it is closely connected with the economics of the rest of the continent (ibid., pp. 62–63)

Chapter Three considers "The method of analysis" and deals with the problem of the role of perception and imagination in sex:

> In the twentieth century the theory of perception has at last achieved the rank of a kind of science ... there are so far two distinct currents of this theory, that merge only at certain points. One is the science of phenomenology, founded by Edmund Husserl; the other is the so-called "Gestalt" or form-psychology. (ibid., p. 67)

Wilson believes that "[h]uman beings possess an *unconscious* will that filters and selects their perceptions" (ibid., p. 74) and that form-imposing mechanisms "blinker" our perceptions, filtering-out rarely experienced visions of "otherness":

> The "doors of perception" all have extremely powerful springs. It is occasionally possible to wedge one of them open for a short period and to let in ... the "otherness" of the world. But they usually slam very quickly, leaving the consciousness imprisoned in its narrow den. (ibid., p. 74)

Wilson sees this principle of the limitation of consciousness as "... the key to the problem of the human sexual impulse" (ibid., p. 77) and feels that "phenomenology might provide a method for temporarily removing the blinkers we all wear on the consciousness" (ibid., p. 74):

> Human beings strive all the time to introduce new elements of "otherness" into their lives. Each new achievement produces a sense of power and opens the door momentarily [but it] closes quickly [and] man is driven on to new efforts of will ... If the *sense* of achievement is more important than the achievement, then men had better learn control of their minds and emotions; by doing so, they might be able to hold on to the sense of achievement longer, or even produce it without long and unnecessary striving. (ibid., p. 75)

There follow Three Chapters on "The meaning of 'perversion'" in which Wilson discusses sadism, fetishism, sex crime, and necrophilia, advocating "… a new avenue of approach to the whole question of sexual perversion … the philosophical rather than the 'pathological' approach" (ibid., p. 78). He suggests that "[i]nstead of asking: Where is the borderline between normality and perversion? We can rephrase the question: What is the permissible limit for human sexual satisfaction?" (ibid., p. 81).

"The sexual experience is the only one from which we are permitted to learn *almost nothing*" (ibid., p. 123), therefore it is necessary to repeat the experience over and over again—"… all these 'perversions' can be regarded as *attempts by individuals to escape the repetition mechanism*" (ibid., p. 122):

> … if the "new existentialism" has a starting point, it is in sex: to devise ways of blocking the repeating mechanism—which at present is as useless to man as a bad stutter—and producing a concept-language for grasping some of the meaning of the sexual experience. (ibid., p. 124)

Wilson feels that "sexual underprivilege" "… is one of the greatest problems of modern civilisation" (ibid., p. 85) and is due largely to a rise in sexual stimulation in western society. "[There is a] certain secret envy of the sexual criminal … and the study of 'imitative' sex crimes reveals the same repressed urge" (ibid., p. 83). This suggests that "… the limitation of consciousness is the villain of the piece" (ibid., p. 82) but should not be seen as a justification of sexual "perversion" or sexual crime, rather a means of understanding it because "… a 'moral judgement' becomes valid if the sexual act involves an invasion of the rights of another person, as in rape and murder …" (ibid., p. 158).

In the next chapter, "Sadism and the criminal mentality", Wilson presents some classic cases of sadistic sex crime and attacks Freudian methods of analysis:

> Freud's error … arises from an employment of an "analytic" instead of Gestalt psychology … these considerations explain why [he] never succeeded in producing a "unifying theory" of sadism. With the libido as the only "ultimate", to which all "aberrated impulses" must be somehow reduced, it is hardly surprising that the problem of sadism should remain impenetrable to Freudian analysis. (ibid., pp. 182–183)

> Because he could not think of sex as an evolutionary urge ... he is left with a barren reduction of all such impulses to the level of the libido. (ibid., p. 181)

He proposes an alternative to the Freudian view:

> It is, to begin with, the need to recognise that the sexual impulse is not the basic human drive ... Freud declared that sex is the universal power-house, and that all other lesser "currents" run off it [but] for the existential psychologist ... the power-house is an evolutionary impulse of ... enormous strength ... (ibid., p. 202)

Whereas "Freud's achievement is incredible", Wilson thinks that "he is still, in many ways, the worst thing that ever happened to the new science of psychology" (ibid., p. 201).

In a section on the problem of sex crime and its punishment, Wilson writes: "... murdering the murderer is no solution. He might still be 'useful' to society if his mentality is carefully studied to determine the psychological and social causes of the crime" (ibid., p. 211). It is interesting to note that, over thirty years later, Wilson was instrumental in persuading Moors Murderer Ian Brady (who was languishing in prison, serving a life sentence) to "... rise above the problem by shifting his mind into creative mode" (Wilson, 2001b, p. 29) and write a book. The result was *The Gates of Janus: Serial Killing and its Analysis*, to which Wilson wrote a long introduction and for which he found a publisher. The book, understandably, caused much controversy and Wilson came under fire from the moral majority but his defence was that it provided an important perspective on serial killers and serial killing that could only be obtained from the "inside".

In the next chapter, "Existential psychology", Wilson continues his attack on Freud:

> What Freud failed to realize is that if a patient is suffering from neurosis, almost any intelligent analysis, under any theory will solve his problems. Often, the patient only needs a "psychological boost" to enable him to make a new effort of prehension, and to solve his own problems ... [He] failed to recognize the importance of "intentionality", of the immense rôle played by the will-power

of the patient. He looked for mechanical causes for the effects, underestimating the freedom and power of human intentionality. (op. cit., p. 220)

He then proceeds to advocate "... the most revolutionary advance in psycho-therapy since the days of William James" (ibid., p. 223), namely the school of existential psychology:

> The whole method of this present book has been phenomenological ... has tried to confine itself to a steady contemplation of "the facts" about sex, without theoretical preconceptions like "conscious and unconscious", the death wish, race-consciousness etc. ... All psychology so far has begun with a set of *preconceptions,* and has made its solution dependent on making the "facts" fit in. (ibid., p. 225)

The final chapter introduces "The theory of symbolic response":

> ... the study of sexual perversion makes it apparent that man can be conditioned to respond sexually to almost anything ... Sex is subjective. By this I mean that there is no necessary relation between the sexual energy and an object ... Sexual response ... is a response to *symbols.* (ibid., p. 242)
>
> ... "inner purpose" *grants reality* to sexual objects and permits a response. There is no external reality, independent of the energy of imagination. Where sex is concerned, there is no "object"; only a symbol clothed with reality by some inner purpose. (ibid., p. 246)
>
> By a phenomenological observation of ourselves and our sexual responses we can ... arrive at a theory of "symbolic response", in which the symbol is invested with meaning by a kind of "grace" of the inner purpose. (ibid., p. 247)

But this "symbolic response" is not just confined to sexual activities: "All aesthetic appreciation is symbolic response" (ibid., p. 247) asserts Wilson, refuting the mechanistic view that all responses depend on what is "out there":

> Except for "consciousness", *the response would not happen at all.* Science continues to investigate the world "out there", and believes that one day ... the universe will be "explained". The theory of

symbolic response declares that even when every inch of the universe "out there" has been mapped and compressed into formulae, the key will still be missing, for the key is "in here"; is an inner-purpose that imposes responses on the outside world. (ibid., p. 249)

And for Wilson "... the aim is and must always be *increase of consciousness*. The immediate problem is the development of methods for extending consciousness into the realms of intentionality" (ibid., pp. 262–263).

An appendix on "The criminal mentality" completes the book.

As was often the case, Wilson attempted to demonstrate that the ideas presented in his non-fiction could be employed in a work of fiction. Thus *The Sex Diary of Gerard Sorme* (aka *Man Without a Shadow: The Diary of an Existentialist*) was released at the same time. This was "an investigation of sex on a fictional level. The first half talks very frankly about his sexual experiences and analyses them. The second half is much more of a novel. He gets mixed up with a character who is based on Aleister Crowley and sees some of his sexual theories put into practice" (Wilson, 1963, n.k.).

* * *

Contemporary critical response to *Origins* ... was not favourable. The psychiatrist Anthony Storr, writing in *The Sunday Times* concluded "[t]hat Mr. Wilson has some ability is evident: but, at present, it is sadly and pretentiously misdirected" (Storr, 1963, n.k.). Maurice Richardson in *The Spectator* called it "the poor man's Kraft-Ebbing" (Richardson, 1963, p. 798). Robert Maurer in *The New York Herald Tribune Books* accused Wilson of "scrapping Freudian theory along with the moral boundaries that traditionally defined sex as normal or abnormal, right or wrong ..." (Maurer, 1963, p. 10) whilst Eric Moon in *The Library Journal* advised librarians that the book should be added to only "... the most bullet-proof and daring of general collections in public libraries" (Moon, 1963, p. 1892). Once again, it seems, Wilson's ideas were ahead of their time. John A. Weigel comments:

Origins ... was variously misread by those whose orthodoxy was offended ... Obviously, Wilson's effect on tender sensibilities had not diminished by 1963. After all, had not the great Freud relegated sex to a comfortably unconscious area of human concerns? Had he not also approved of the suppression of sexual impulses as a means of motivating creativity via sublimation? Freud was a true prophet, but Wilson was a heretic! Today's heresies, however, often become tomorrow's truths. Wilson begins to find comfort in being a heretic ... (Weigel, 1975, p. 57)

Clifford P. Bendau adds:

Origins ... takes the *Outsider Cycle* one step further into the existential study of man [attempting] to understand the role and function of sex in the structure of "man's total being" ... Whether Wilson ever intended to formulate a grand theory of sexuality for its own sake is doubtful. What is most important to Wilson's overall thesis is the idea of the intentionality of consciousness. In this light, *Origins* ... is closely aligned with his writings on the evolutionary purposiveness of life. (Bendau, 1979, p. 37)

As ever, undaunted, Wilson "went back to work more eagerly than ever" (Weigel, 1975, p. 57) and completed his "Outsider Cycle" with the next volume, *Beyond the Outsider: The Philosophy of the Future* (1965) and its summary volume *Introduction to the New Existentialism* (1966). He returned to the subject of sex soon after with a book of sexual advice for young people: *Sex and the Intelligent Teenager* (1966), and another novel about sex: *The God of the Labyrinth*, aka *The Hedonists* (1970).

New Pathways in Psychology: Maslow and the Post-Freudian Revolution (1972)

This book marks Wilson's brief return to his original publisher Victor Gollancz after an absence of nine years. It was published in the UK in May 1972 and in the US by Taplinger Publishing Company the same year. In an article written to promote a new book, *Super Consciousness* (see Chapter Nine), in 2009, Colin Wilson wrote:

> One day in the spring of 1963 I received one of the most important letters of my life. It was from a professor of psychology named Abraham Maslow, and he wanted to tell me about some researches he had been carrying out for the past ten years or so.

This, written nearly forty years after Maslow's death in 1970, reveals how important Wilson considers his association with the American psychologist has been and how much it has helped to reinforce his own ideas about the nature of human consciousness. It was, as the extract suggests, Maslow who made the initial contact:

> Four years after the publication of my book *The Age of Defeat*—under the title *The Stature of Man*—I had received a letter from Maslow. ...

He explained that he had been impressed by the optimism of *The Stature of Man*, and about the way I had pinpointed the sense of defeat that permeates our culture.

Maslow had begun to have certain doubts about Freudian psychology, feeling it had "sold human nature short". This was something I had felt strongly for years: Freud's view that all our deepest urges are sexual seemed to me to leave out some of the most important members of the human race, from Leonardo to Bernard Shaw ... (Wilson, 2003, p. 208)

The book is divided into three parts, with a lengthy introductory chapter outlining the ideas that Wilson and Maslow have in common. Part one provides a history of the major trends in psychology from its beginnings, through Sigmund Freud (1856–1939) to Maslow. Part two deals exclusively with Maslow and part three discusses existential psychology in general.

In the introduction, Wilson explains why he considers Maslow's concept of "peak experiences" (PEs)—that sudden rush of pure happiness that we all experience in moments of delight—to be so important and asks whether they can be induced. Maslow felt that this was not possible but Wilson believes that PEs have "... a structure that can be duplicated. It is the culmination of a series of mental acts, each of which can be clearly defined" (Wilson, 1972, p. 21). The basis of the PE is a state of "... vigilance, alertness, *preparedness* ..." (ibid., p. 22) and "... the first pre-condition is 'energy', because the PE is essentially an overflowing of energy" (ibid., p. 21). In one of his typical analogies, Wilson sees healthy people as having surplus energy stored in their subconscious minds: "... like money that has been invested in stocks and shares" (ibid., p. 22). Near the surface of the subconscious mind some of this energy is stored ready for use "... like money in a personal account" (ibid., p. 22). When a delightful event is anticipated large quantities of surplus energy are made available for use:

> ... as I might draw a large sum out of the bank before I go on holiday ... Peakers are people with large quantities of energy in the ready energy tanks. Bored or miserable people are people who keep only small amounts of energy for immediate use. (ibid., p. 22)

However, both types of people have the same amounts of energy available to them: "... it is merely a matter of transferring it to your 'current account'" (ibid., p. 22).

Both Maslow and Wilson see the need for us to live meaningful creative lives: "Meaning stimulates the will, fills one with a desire to reach out to new horizons" (ibid., p. 26). The PE is a sudden surge of meaning and "the question that arises now is: how can I *choose* meaning?" (ibid., p. 26). Wilson thinks that the secret lies in concentration and introduces an exercise which he later called "the pen trick":

> ... I discovered that a mild peak experience could easily be induced merely by concentrating hard on a pencil, then relaxing the attention, then concentrating again ... After doing this a dozen or so times, the attention becomes fatigued—if you are doing it with the right degree of concentration—and a few more efforts—deliberately ignoring the fatigue—trigger the peak experience. After all, concentration has the effect of summoning energy from your depths. It is the "pumping" motion—of expanding and contracting the attention—that causes the peak experience. (ibid., pp. 29–30)

(In his book *Access to Inner Worlds* (see Chapter Six), Wilson describes how he taught this trick to a class of students, combining it with a breathing exercise devised by Wilhelm Reich (1897–1957): "After a few moments, I noticed the curious sense of exaltation, followed by a sensation as if floating out of my body ... Time became unimportant ... we had been lying there for more than half an hour, and ... no one showed the slightest inclination to get up" (Wilson, 1983, p. 38)).

Wilson highlights the importance of human imagination that, in most cases, only provides a poor copy of the original experience. The exception, however, is sex, where the imagination can carry men and women to the point of sexual climax, achieving "a physical response *as if* to reality" (op. cit., p. 30). He feels that it should be possible for imagination to achieve this result, not just with sex, but in all fields.

In this chapter Wilson also introduces "... a concept that has become the core of my own existential psychology: the 'Self-Image'" (ibid., p. 34), that is, the way we view ourselves. This is a notion "of immediate relevance to Maslovian psychology" (ibid., p. 37) because boosting one's self-image can lead to the "promotion of the personality to a higher level" (ibid., p. 35). It achieves this by providing a sense of external meaning. But, if this meaning is always there, why do I not experience it all the time?

> ... because I allow the will to become passive, and the senses close up. If I want more meaning, then I must force my senses wide open by an increased effort of will. We might think of the senses as spring-loaded shutters that must be forced open, and which close again when you let them go ... If I am not careful, the shutters close and I lose my objective standards. At this point I may wildly exaggerate the importance of my emotions, my private ups and downs, and there is no feeling of objective reality to contradict me. (ibid., p. 37)

(As usual, Wilson also attempted to convey his ideas in the form of a novel. The self-image concept is central to his 1985 novel *The Personality Surgeon* in which the hero invents a revolutionary form of psychotherapy, involving the use of a video camera and digital paintbox, with the intention of improving the patient's self-image. Wilson speaks of the self-image concept on the CD *The Essential Colin Wilson*. In the sleeve notes he writes: "I always intended to write a book called *The Self Image*, but never got round to it. Before a human being can live a creative and fruitful existence, he must have *a clear idea who he is*. It is as if we were all in need of a *mirror* in which we could see our own faces. Nietzsche meant the same thing when he said: 'The great man is the play actor of his own ideals'" (Wilson, 1986b)).

"'Reality' is the key word in existential psychology," (op. cit., p. 40) writes Wilson. We can always re-establish contact with reality by "an effort of reaching out to meaning" (ibid., p. 41):

> And the most important point for psychotherapy is that [we] can do this *by an act of will*. Mental illness is a kind of amnesia, in which the patient has forgotten his own powers. The task of the therapist is to somehow renew the patient's contact with reality. (ibid., p. 41)

In part one, Chapter One, "The age of machinery: from Descartes to Mill", Wilson writes: "It is one of the absurd paradoxes of psychology that it has taken three centuries to reach the conclusion that man actually possesses a mind and a will" (ibid., p. 47). Starting with

René Descartes (1596–1650) and progressing through Thomas Hobbes (1588–1679), John Locke (1632–1704), and David Hume (1711–1776), he traces how this came about. He considers Hume to be "one of the most significant figures in the history of psychology. For Hume's model of the human mind, has influenced every psychologist—directly or otherwise—since the publication of *A Treatise of Human Nature* (1739)" (ibid., p. 49). Wilson attacks his theory that thinking and willing are illusions. "One stage further, and he will be assuring me that I am not alive at all, and that there is no such thing as consciousness" (ibid., p. 50).

This mechanistic view of man's mind was perpetuated by James Mill (1773–1836) and in spite of the work of Hermann Lotze (1817–1881) "and various other psychologists who accepted the reality of the will, psychology remained mechanistic" (ibid., p. 60):

> ... by ... the late 19th and early 20th centuries ... the great Freudian revolution was under way. ... There seemed to be a general feeling that since psychology had attained the rank of a science, it had better stick to analysis and definition. The will ... was allowed a small place among feelings, cognitions, memories, and so on, but it had to take its place at the back of the queue. (ibid., p. 60)

Part one, Chapter Two, "Towards a psychology of the will: from Brentano to James", concentrates on the work of Franz Brentano (1838–1917) and his pupil Edmund Husserl (1859–1938) whose concept of the intentionality of perception is central to Wilson's own ideas. In contrast to Hume they insisted that thoughts and feelings were always about things; in effect they *reach out* to things. "It is intentional. I look *at* something: that is, I do half the work" (ibid., p. 63). This begs the question: "If thoughts are not blown around like leaves on a windy day, but directed by a sense of purpose, then who does the directing?" (ibid., p. 62). The answer is the transcendental ego. "But ... the intentional element in perception—the part *I* put into it—often distorts what my senses convey" (ibid., p. 63). So, according to Wilson, Husserl's basic assertion could be summarised as follows:

> Philosophy has no chance of making a true statement about any-thing until it can distinguish between what the senses really *tell* us—the undistorted perception—and how we interpret it. ... The

> philosophical method that Husserl called "pure phenomenology"
> is an attempt to teach the mind to be objective. (ibid., p. 64)

The rest of the chapter is devoted to the American philosopher and psychologist William James (1842–1910) who "… discovered the concept of intentionality at about the same time as Husserl, but made less practical use of it in his philosophy" (ibid., p. 65). However, Wilson considers that he "… has provided more insights into the actual working of the human mind than any other psychologist or philosopher" (ibid., p. 71) and feels that his *Varieties of Religious Experience* (1902) "… may well be the most important single volume in the history of psychology, since it is a direct attack on the problem of man's spiritual evolution" (ibid., p. 81).

> But although James asserted that there can be no psychological
> proof of free will, he nevertheless goes straight to the heart of the
> matter when he points out that we become aware of free will when
> we are *making an effort*. (ibid., p. 68)

This is an important point, one that Wilson emphasises again and again throughout his work:

> In order to grasp meanings, I must "focus"—concentrate, "contract" my attention muscles. Perception is intentional, and the more
> energy (or effort) I put into the act of "concentrating", the more
> meaning I grasp. (ibid., p. 68)

Most human beings, says Wilson, spend much of their lives with their attention "… vague, broad, diffused, unfocused, like a bored schoolboy staring blankly out of a window …" (ibid., p. 68). It is only when faced with some crisis or emergency that they snap out of their dream:

> Without emergency to keep them "on their toes", their general level
> of intensity diminishes; they take their comfort for granted; their
> responses become dulled. And, in a vague, distressed way they
> wonder what went wrong, why life is suddenly so unexciting. …
> Why has life failed?
>   This is one of the most urgent problems for civilised man. (ibid.,
> p. 68)

With these statements we arrive at the heart of Wilson's message: "There is something wrong with 'normal' human consciousness. For some odd reason, we seldom get the best out of it" (ibid., p. 87). The answer, he thinks, lies in higher levels of consciousness: "The higher one ascends on this scale, the more *self-sustaining* consciousness becomes" (ibid., p. 69). In this sense Maslow's preoccupation with creativity is seen as a logical step beyond James and Husserl. However, "[i]t is ironical," writes Wilson, "that after [James'] death in 1910, psychology should have been dominated by a new kind of determinism, that had no place for 'will' or 'values'" (ibid., p. 87).

The first chapter of part two delivers a biographical sketch of Maslow based on several tapes prepared by Maslow himself and sent to Wilson, after his death in 1970, by his widow Bertha:

> The paradox about Maslow is not simply that he was a reluctant rebel, but that he was unwilling to regard himself as any kind of rebel at all. ... He saw himself as a psychoanalyst and a behaviour-ist, not as the father of a revolution against them. He was a creative synthesiser, not in the least interested in dissension; this was his own way of making the best of his creative energies. (ibid., p. 130)

The second chapter of part two is an account of the development of Maslow's ideas, commencing with his studies of monkey behaviour in the 1930s from which "[h]e had evolved a new theory of evolution ..., with dominance playing the central role, rather than sexual selection ..." (ibid., p. 157). He then went on to try and discover whether there was a close correlation between sexuality and dominance in human beings. It was in a paper, "A theory of human motivation", published in the *Psychological Review* in July 1943 that he first proposed his important theory of the "hierarchy of needs": "What Maslow stated in this paper is the essence of his life work" (ibid., p. 162), writes Wilson:

> Maslow's theory, then, is that there are five levels of needs: physiological, safety, love, esteem and self-actualisation, and as one becomes satisfied, another takes over. ... The really revolutionary point here ... was that these "higher needs" are as instinctoid as the lower, as much part of man's subconscious drives. (ibid., pp. 163–164)

(In a fascinating article on criminology, "A doomed society?", Wilson described how these levels correspond roughly to periods of crime: "Until the first part of the 19th century, most crimes were committed out of a need for food and security. Then came the age of sex crime." Finally, "the self-esteem motive might explain more recent 'gratuitous' murders" (Wilson, 1973a, pp. 395–410)).

Maslow's paper on self-actualising people, written in 1950 and later included in the book *Motivation and Personality* (1954; revised 1970), is described by Wilson as

> ... probably Maslow's most important single work. ... It is revolutionary because this is the first time a psychologist has ignored the assumption that underlies all Freudian psychology: that psychology, like medicine, is basically a study of the sick ... (ibid., p. 171)

Maslow discovered that a great many of these healthy self-actualisers

> ... have peak experiences, mystical experiences, "the oceanic feeling", the sense of limitless horizons opening up to the vision. In the first edition of *Motivation and Personality* in 1954, Maslow speaks only of mystical experiences and the oceanic feeling; in the 1970 edition—issued after his death—he uses the term "peak experience". (ibid., p. 171)

He was puzzled, however, by the fact that affluence does not project *everyone* toward self-actualisation. Wilson suggests that this is because it requires

> ... a different *kind* of development. ... Ordinary development can take place on a horizontal level; self-actualisation requires a kind of vertical movement. ... The gap between ordinary human passivity and the active freedom involved in creation is absolute, as different as real activity is from dreaming. (ibid., p. 201)

So, despite the other needs—physiological, safety, love, esteem—being satisfied, human passivity is a bar to further development:

> What was really needed, to complete Maslow's theory, was the realisation developed by [Victor] Frankl [1905–1997] a decade

later—that when human beings are passive, *neurosis tends to feed upon itself.* ... Neurosis, says Maslow, is a failure of personal growth. Frankl adds that healthy activity demands a goal, a sense of something worth doing, and that mental illness begins when men are deprived of the sense of "something to look forward to". Boredom, passivity, stagnation: these are the beginning of mental illness, which propagates itself like scum on a stagnant pond. (ibid., pp. 172 & 174)

Summarising Maslow's achievement, Wilson states:

> Like all original thinkers, he has opened up a new way of *seeing* the universe. His ideas developed slowly and organically ...; there are no breaks, or sudden changes of direction. His instinct is remarkably sound; none of his work has been disproved; none has had to be re-done ...; in fact, I can see no single example in which he was definitely mistaken. He advanced with the faultless precision of a sleepwalker. (ibid., p. 198)

In part three, Wilson asks the question "Where now?" and further examines the work of Frankl, along with that of Ludwig Binswanger (1881–1966), Medard Boss (1903–1990), Erwin Straus (1891–1975), Roberto Assagioli (1888–1974), Rollo May (1909–1994), R. D. Laing (1927–1989), and G. I. Gurdjieff (1866–1949) whose "... importance in the history of psychology is not recognised; but as the 'existential' revolution proceeds, he is bound to become known as one of the greatest originators of the twentieth century" (ibid., p. 209). He also considers the "reality therapy" of William Glasser (1925-) and the "attitude therapy" of Dan MacDougald (dates unknown).

> There is one obvious difference between the new movement in psychology—the trends and theories that can be loosely grouped together as "existential"—and the older schools of Freud, Jung, Adler and Rank. The existential school adopts a more down-to-earth, empirical approach to mental illness. There is a notable absence of dogmatic underpinning, theories about the subconscious and its hypothetical contents. The psychiatrist tends to approach the patient with an attitude of self-identification: "How could I myself get into that condition?" And, obviously,

the answer will be in terms of conscious pressures. (ibid., p. 213)

Wilson observes that man is not naturally static: "His mental being must be understood as something essentially dynamic, forward-flowing, like a river ..." (ibid., p. 220). This flow is

> ... not the Freudian libido or the Adlerian will to power, but a *sense of values* which operates rather like radar, by a kind of "reaching out" ... *Man is future-orientated*, not sex-orientated or power-orientated. ... What man craves is not power, but objective reality, values beyond himself. (ibid., p. 220)

"The central need at the moment," writes Wilson, "is to develop a psychology of man's higher consciousness, a complete breakaway from Freudian pathology" (ibid., p. 252). He introduces his own "control psychology":

> The basic human problem is to maintain continually the state in which peak experiences are possible. This means, in practical terms, a certain forward-drive, and a deep seated refusal to accept depression, discouragement, all the various shades of defeat. We have got to realise that the "pressure" we live at is too low to allow the development of our evolutionary potentialities. (ibid., p. 247)

So we need to "tighten-up" the controls. When we do this "... the world seems *more real*. New meanings appear. And it is the act of concentration *itself* that causes this intensification of consciousness" (ibid., p. 245). For Wilson, this is an important point: meaning does not just come from "out there", it has to be met with the full force of our attention.

In the last section of this long chapter, Wilson attempts to take the first steps towards creating a phenomenology for the new psychology. His starting point is the intentionality of consciousness. However:

> ... consciousness is also *relational* by nature. ... [J]ust as perception depends upon a subjective "reaching out" towards the object, so the object-as-perceived is not a simple thing, but a complex structure depending on the relation between the object and the rest of the contents of consciousness. (ibid., p. 256)

> ... it is important to recognise that *all* perception involves a sense
> of relations, just as all perception involves intentionality. ... Nothing
> can be perceived in true isolation; all perception is relational.
>
> Relationality is the meaning experience; intentionality is the will
> experience. They are intimately related, in that relationality can be
> increased by an act of intentionality, and meaning, in turn, stimu-
> lates and guides intention. (ibid., p. 257)

This, according to Wilson, proves Maslow is right about his "oceanic
feeling" being proof of "higher ceilings for human nature". "When we
recognise that perception must be both intentional and relational, then
the 'oceanic feeling' is seen to be a wider state of relationality" (ibid.,
p. 257).

But if perception is seen as an arrow fired towards its target, the bow-
string needs to be taut. With effort, says Wilson, we can learn to do this
but first we must restrain what he calls our "Robot" from doing our
perceiving for us. "[The] Robot is a labour-saving device. ... When an
activity has been performed often enough, he takes over and ... does it a
great deal more efficiently than I could do it consciously. ... Whenever I
acquire some new skill, it gives me pleasure, but the moment the Robot
takes over, the pleasure vanishes. ... The consequence is that when life
is peaceful, we find it difficult to feel really alive ..." (Wilson, 1970b,
pp. 38–40). Also, a strong self-image, is seen to be important: "We might
consider psychotherapy as a process of encouraging the patient to seek
for a suitable self-image—one that is consistent with the highest level of
self-esteem and creativity" (op. cit., p. 267).

> The importance of this—for post-Maslow psychology—is immense.
> It means that *anybody* can become a "peaker". Provided they are
> willing to put a certain amount of effort into it. Non-peakers are
> either the habitually lazy or the habitually *discouraged*—those who
> do not realise how easy it is to become a peaker. (ibid., p. 266)

* * *

Contemporary reviews were, as usual, extreme. Alan Hull-Walton
wrote:

> Here is no fuddy-duddy "head shrunk" psychologist abiding by
> the rules and regulations of the enclosed academic establishment,

but a man who has read and studied deeply, and is not afraid to
say what he believes to be the truth. ... His superlative technique
of breaking new ground in a controlled, concise, and easy prose, is
absolutely incredible ... (Walton, 1972, p. 50)

Whereas the anonymous reviewer in *British Book News* (July 1972,
p. 551) asks: "Colin Wilson's edifice upon Maslow's foundation is a
provocative and interesting construction, but is it architecture or con-
fectionery?" The psychologist Charles Rycroft (1914–1998) obviously
thought the latter: "If there were, as there should be, an annual prize for
the most pretentious and unscholarly book of the year, Colin Wilson's
latest effusion would certainly be the winner for 1972", although he
later reluctantly admits that, despite all this, Wilson may be "... on
to something" (Rycroft, 1972, pp. 818–819). In a rather "light-weight"
review, considering the subject matter, Herbert Lomas declared: "It's
not that one disagrees in general with his phenomenological premises;
it's his vulgarization of them" (Lomas, 1972, pp. 148–149). In America,
a rather more considered appraisal was provided by James S. Gordon in
the *New York Times Book Review* (Jan 28, 1973, pp. 2–3) who nevertheless
accused Wilson of smuggling into the book "... a naïve essentialism in
the guise of existential theory ...".

John A. Weigel comments:

> Wilson's goal as prophetic philosopher is more clearly defined than
> ever in his book-length exploration of the importance of certain
> psychological insights. ... *New Pathways in Psychology*, is an open-
> ended summary of what Colin Wilson is all about. Students, critics,
> and others interested in Wilson are well advised to make use of its
> select bibliography, index, heuristic summaries, case studies, and
> suggestions for research along these new pathways. (Weigel, 1975,
> p. 133)

Clifford P. Bendau sees the book as

> ... much more than a text on Maslow. *Pathways* represents an exten-
> sive survey of the history of psychology [and is] an accumulation
> of Colin Wilson's ideas on the topic of psychology and the future of
> man. ... It is important ... because Wilson uses this opportunity to
> update his early ideas ... (Bendau, 1979, pp. 54–55)

Finally, in his chapter on Wilson's psychology, Howard F. Dossor concludes:

> The existential psychology that Wilson embraces is one of the most exciting theories ever to have been created by the human mind. ... It makes all other psychologies appear inadequate because it is a profound synthesis of the best that each of them has to offer ... (Dossor, 1990, p. 113)

CHAPTER FOUR

Frankenstein's Castle: The Right Brain— Door to Wisdom (1980)

This short book (128 pages in length) was first published by Ashgrove Press (Bath, UK), in the US and the UK, in 1980. The first edition appeared in hardback and paperback with the subtitle *The Double Brain: Door to Wisdom* on the title page and *The Right Brain: Door to Wisdom* on the cover. The title page was changed to the latter on subsequent editions. A Japanese translation by Hirakawa Shuppan-Sha (Mind Books) of Tokyo was published in 1984.

Here Wilson applies the results of split-brain research (which was carried out in the US by Joseph Bogen (1926–2005), Michael Gazzaniga (1939-), and the Nobel laureate Roger Sperry (1913–1994), and their associates and students, in the early 1960s and became *the* fashionable field in neuroscience) to his ideas on human consciousness. Wilson apparently discovered this research in the mid-1970s and first made mention of it in the second of his "Occult Trilogy" books *Mysteries: an Investigation into the Occult, the Paranormal and the Supernatural* (1978).

Chapter One, "The 'other mode'" was considered important enough to be included by Wilson in the 1985 compilation *The Essential Colin Wilson*. It commences with Wilson asserting that his "… life has been dominated by a single obsession: a search for what I call 'the other mode of consciousness'" (Wilson, 1991, p. 13). This "other mode" can be experienced by all of us as "a feeling of wild happiness, a rising tide of sheer exhilaration" (ibid., p. 13). The American professor of psychology Abraham Maslow called these brief flashes "peak experiences" but he insisted that they just happened and could not be repeated at will. Wilson, however, sees them as "a product of vitality and optimism" which can "be amplified or repeated through *reflection*, by turning the full attention upon it" (ibid., p. 16). In this way "the 'other mode' *is* within our control" (ibid., p. 17). Wilson feels that the reason we experience these moments of clarity infrequently is due to the influence of what he calls "the robot" (the mechanical part of us that does difficult tasks without us having to think about them). A very necessary and useful tool, "the robot" unfortunately "also gets 'used to' spring mornings and Mozart symphonies, destroying 'the glory and freshness' that makes the child's world so interesting" (ibid., p. 17). So how can we achieve this clarity of vision, this "primal perception"? The answer lies within our brains and Wilson believes the secret is revealed by studying the results of split-brain research.

In Chapter Two, Wilson suggests that we have, in effect, two brains, which he likens to Frankenstein's Castle in Germany which was split into two parts and owned by two different families in the fourteenth century:

> The person you call "you" lives in the left side of your brain. And a few centimetres away there is another person, a completely independent identity. ... In effect the left-brain person is a scientist, the right-brain an artist. (ibid., p. 21)
>
> The business of the left is to "cope" with everyday problems. The business of the right is to deal with our inner-states and feelings. (ibid., p. 25)

It seems, however, that the right brain is in charge of our energy supply. When we are tired we only need to become absorbed in something to feel the energy come flowing back. So what is the secret of persuading the right brain to grant us more energy? "If we can discover this," writes Wilson, "we have discovered the secret of the 'other mode'—and probably the secret of human evolution" (ibid., p. 26).

Wilson suggests that the root of all neuroses can be traced to the conflict of left and right brain "egos": the left being the master of consciousness, the right the master of the unconscious. He sees their relationship to be similar to that of Stan Laurel and Oliver (Ollie)

Hardy in the old Hollywood films. This theory of Wilson's first appeared in print as an essay entitled "Consciousness and the divided brain", published in the journal *Second Look* (volume 1, no. 12) in October 1979. It was reprinted as "The Laurel and Hardy theory of consciousness" in *The Essential Colin Wilson* and eventually as a booklet in 1986. Ollie, the dominant, bossy type, is the left and Stan, the vague and childlike character, the right. Stan always takes his cues from Ollie. If Ollie is cheerful, Stan is ecstatic; if Ollie is feeling gloomy, Stan becomes depressed (he always overreacts). It is Stan, however, who controls the vital energy which he provides in abundance when Ollie is in a positive state of mind. But when Stan becomes depressed, the energy is blocked, Ollie becomes even gloomier, and we find ourselves caught in a downward spiral of negative feedback. The "other mode", however, depends upon communication between the two brains resulting in *"positive* feedback":

> If I experience some enormous relief, as some appalling threat is removed, Ollie gives a sigh of contentment, and Stan reacts by sending up a wave of relief. And suddenly, Ollie is seeing things in a completely new way—grass looks greener, everything is somehow "more interesting". (ibid., p. 29)

This widening of awareness is the key to the "other mode" bringing a sense that "all is well"; the problem, however, is that we spend a great deal of our time habitually narrowing our attention, suffocated by a sense of mistrust and inadequacy. This provides us with a "worm's eye" rather than a "bird's eye" view of life:

> The business of the right-brain is pattern recognition, the "bird's eye view". The left-brain is confined to the "worm's eye view". Where over-all patterns and meanings are concerned, a bird's eye view undoubtedly provides a truer picture than the worm's. So we conclude that the sense of "absurd good news", the feeling that "all is well", *is* justified. (ibid., p. 37)

In Chapter Three, Wilson warns us against considering the left brain as a villain:

> The two halves need to combine their functions. When this happens, the result is far greater than either could achieve

individually. ... the faculties of the right and left hemispheres, of insight and logic, can be focused together. ... When this happens, the result is a *sense of actuality*, as if the mind had suddenly "got the distance" between itself and the real world. For this sense of actuality I have suggested the term "Faculty X". (ibid., p. 48)

Asserting that the fundamental human urge is *not* for happiness, but for control, Wilson insists that "the most important element in Faculty X is not the 'insight', but the discipline and control of the 'left-brain'" (ibid., p. 48). But Faculty X moments are rare due to our senses being dulled by habit:

> ... the real problem of human existence ... is this power of habit to *rob us of all sense of reality*. In this sense we are all dual personalities; for half the time we are striving and struggling to stay alive and improve our lot; the other half, we accept the present as if there was no reality beyond it, and lapse into a kind of hypnotic trance. (ibid., p. 49)

Wilson argues that psychologically speaking, we consist of three major components: the left brain, the right brain, and the "robot" and that these actively interfere with one another to such an extent that the necessary alliance between our "robot" and the left brain, in order to guarantee our survival, has robbed us of this sense of reality: "What it means, then, is that human beings possess a possibility ... of *breaking through* to a new evolutionary level of vision and purpose" (ibid., p. 54). All we need to do is solve the problem of this interference (The "robot" can form an alliance with the right brain too, with unfortunate consequences, as Wilson points-out later).

In Chapter Four, Wilson advises against the use of drugs to achieve right-brain awareness:

> ... their effects are not controllable. Ideally, we should be able to move freely between left- and right-brain consciousness. Too much left-brain consciousness may be bad for us, but to put it out of action with mescalin is like swatting a fly with a sledgehammer. Less violent methods are required. (ibid., p. 60)

Methods of inducing right-brain awareness—bio-feedback, meditation, yoga—come closer to the solution because they involve conscious control but they produce a *passive* type of "peak experience". Wilson argues for an *active* "peak experience": "Man is fundamentally a problem-solver ... we are at our best when overcoming obstacles, breaking down barriers" (ibid., p. 66). What is required is a subtle movement of our personal centre of gravity to the right so that we can achieve freedom from the hypertensions of the left. Too much to the right and we enter into the realms of mysticism and lose touch with our left brain altogether:

> ... this "other mode" of consciousness is not in any way remote from everyday consciousness; it lies right at the side of it, only a fraction of a millimetre away. It is seen, like a lightning flash, in all moments of joy and relief, as our *deliberately limited* left-brain perception is replaced by a wider pattern. (ibid., p. 69)

In Chapter Five, "The power of the right", Wilson reveals that the differing functions of the two hemispheres was known about as far back as 1893 when Thomson J. Hudson (1834–1903) wrote his book *The Law of Psychic Phenomena*. He suggests that the powers of the right brain are such that they may be responsible for many so-called "occult" phenomena: telepathy, calculating prodigies, multiple personalities, poltergeists, etc.

> The only thing that seems perfectly clear is that the "other being" who inhabits Frankenstein's Castle is a miracle worker. ... No doubt the reason he can perform these feats is that no one has ever explained to him that they are impossible. (ibid., p. 84)

In the penultimate chapter, "Clues", Wilson, once again, introduces the personal element that characterises much of his work, "brings it to life" as it were, and demonstrates that his theories can work in practice. Recalling an incident from his youth, he shows how the alliance between the *right* brain and the robot can lead to disaster:

> These two form a purely mechanical alliance. Instinct assesses the urgency of a situation, the robot places that judgement on

permanent record, and from then on, decides whether a certain effort is *worth* making. ... [this] alliance keeps us *trapped* at a certain level of mechanicalness. It tells me that the day ahead of me is going to be fairly uninteresting, and that therefore I need make no particular effort. (ibid., p. 101)

This, asserts Wilson, is why we need the left-brain ego: to overrule instinct and the robot and make us see that *no* day is uninteresting and to stop us from wasting our lives in mechanical repetition.

In the final chapter, "Discoveries", Wilson puts the case for a "transcendental ego", as proposed by Edmund Husserl (1859–1938): "... some kind of 'self' that presides over consciousness and directs the act of thinking" (ibid., p. 106). He concludes that this "self" is, in fact, the *left-brain ego* but: "... trapped in its narrow conceptual consciousness, overawed by the enormous mechanisms of the brain and body, the 'presiding ego' fails to realise that it ought to be in control ..." (ibid., p. 109). Only in emergencies does it remember that it is in charge. "Our real problem," explains Wilson, "is that neurotic tendency of the left-ego to isolate itself from the powers of the right, and then forget that these powers are at its disposal ..." (ibid., p. 113). Art can remind us of these powers but is "not the solution we are looking for" (ibid., p. 113). Wilson concludes that: "Once you know that 'you' should be in control of consciousness, and you make a determined effort in that direction, the rest follows inevitably" (ibid., p. 123). After "a few days of constant effort" (ibid., p. 128) he sees left-brain consciousness as not so much an "observer" but more a *gatherer of power*: "And that is what the left-brain was intended for. Its far-sightedness gives it the ability to summon power" (ibid., p. 128).

He likens Man's current situation to someone who possesses a magic machine that can produce an unlimited amount of gold coins; enough to abolish world poverty. But because he fears the machine might empty he only produces enough coins to see him through the day. "The fear is unnecessary," insists Wilson. "It is magical, and cannot be emptied" (ibid., p. 128).

* * *

As always, with a book from Wilson, critical response was extreme. David Loshak wrote:

This is a short book but few of greater length could be so studded with illumination, allusion and the stuff of scientific controversy … Agree or not with its many provocative insights, it well repays reading, thinking over and reading again. (Loshak, 1981, p. 63)

Stuart Sutherland did not agree. Feeling that Wilson constantly "misuses technical terms", he suggested that the author "would do better to place more reliance on a good dictionary and less on his right hemisphere". He clearly didn't read to the end of the book, however, because he claimed that Wilson "gives no guidance to readers on how to keep the two sides of their brains in cahoots" (Sutherland, 1981, n.k.).

Tom Greenwell, in a somewhat tongue-in-cheek review stated:

Colin Wilson does not just write books; he shares experiences with readers. He uses ideas—good ones, bad ones; new ones, old ones—as a climber uses footholds and handholds to zig-zag his way to the ultimate goal. Sometimes Mr. Wilson falters, slips back a bit, and finds new paths around obstacles; but the general progress is upwards and towards the sunlight. (Greenwell, 1981, n.k.)

Regarding Wilson's "Laurel and Hardy theory of consciousness", he noted that: "It is more fun to see Stan as a Right Charlie than as a Right Brain."

Howard F. Dossor, in a more sober vein, saw Wilson's existential psychology as

… one of the most exciting theories ever to have been created by the human mind. It is the product of an alert intelligence cooperating with a sharp intuition. It has about it a sense that it is as much given as created. It provides a satisfying explanation of the path we have traversed in the past; of our present frustration and of the way forward. (Dossor, 1990, p. 113)

CHAPTER FIVE

The Quest for Wilhelm Reich (1981)

It was inevitable that Colin Wilson would become interested in Wilhelm Reich (1897–1957) at some stage, for he was, very much, the "outsider" of the psychoanalytic movement. He first mentioned Reich in his classic 1971 study *The Occult* (1971). In the same year his essay entitled "Freud, Reich and Nietzsche" was published in *The Humanist* (July 1971, pp. 213–214) and an extended book review, "Wilhelm Reich's sex and psychology", appeared a year later in *Books & Bookmen* (August 1972, pp. 18–21). This review was published in its own right as the eleven-page pamphlet *Wilhelm Reich* in 1974 and included in the booklet *Hesse–Reich–Borges* (1974). In the latter he mentioned that he was currently researching a book on Reich. That book, *The Quest for Wilhelm Reich*, appeared in 1981, published by Granada Publishing Ltd. in the UK and Anchor Press/Doubleday in the US with a UK paperback edition a year later; Spanish and Japanese translations were also, at various times, available.

In a prefatory note, Wilson explained the problems he had obtaining permission to quote from Reich's work. Whereas Reich's American publishers granted permission free of charge, his UK publisher, Vision Press, requested that Wilson, by way of payment, contribute to a symposium they were publishing called *The Art of Emily Brontë*. He complied and his essay "A personal response to *Wuthering Heights*" appeared in that volume (edited by Anne Smith) in 1976. That was not the end of the story, however, for, during the course of his research, Wilson learned from previous Reich biographers that permission to quote had also to be sought from Reich's executor, Mary Boyd Higgins. Because his book contained a certain amount of criticism of Reich and his work, permission was refused, forcing Wilson to restrict his quotations to the length permitted by the copyright laws.

In his introduction, Wilson outlined how he became interested in Reich after buying a second-hand copy of *The Cancer Biopathy* (1948) in the mid-1960s. But when he tried to find out more about Reich's life it proved difficult: "His books contain fragments of autobiography, but there is a curious underlying feeling of inhibition and reticence" (Wilson, 1982, p. 6). Then, in 1969, *Wilhelm Reich: A Personal Biography* (London: Elek), written by his third wife, Ilsa Ollendorff Reich, was published and Wilson "… became fascinated by this enigma of a scientist turning, against his will, into a metaphysical philosopher" (ibid., p. 6). His reading convinced him that Reich was a classic example of the psychological type "The Right Man": men who "… under no circumstances could … acknowledge the possibility that they might be in the wrong" (ibid., p. 7). This was a theory expounded by the science fiction writer A(lfred) E(lton) van Vogt (1912–2000) in an essay entitled *A Report on the Violent Male* (1975, 1992):

> Ilse Ollendorff's biography made it clear that Reich became a highly developed example of the Right Man type. (She mentions, for example, his pathological jealousy: "… he would accuse [me] of infidelity with any man who came to his mind as a possible rival, whether colleague, friend, local shopkeeper or casual acquaintance.") (ibid., p. 9)

Despite his dislike of Reich's personality, Wilson, whilst writing about the theories of Anton Mesmer (1734–1815) and Baron Karl von Reichenbach (1788–1869) in *The Occult*, felt that there was a certain correlation with Reich's idea of orgone energy. Intrigued, he continued his research, seeking out and interviewing the Reichian therapist Robert Ollendorff (Ilse's brother), Ilse Ollendorff herself, Reich's friend the educator A. S. Neill (1883–1973), and Constance Rooth-Tracey, a patient of Reich's. In Robert Ollendorff's consulting room Wilson was able to sit inside one of Reich's orgone boxes:

> It was a large box, about half the size of a telephone booth. The walls were roughly six inches thick, made of alternating layers of metal and asbestos. ... There was a large hole in the door, about a foot square, through which I could look when I was seated on the chair inside the box. Ollendorff took my temperature before I went inside; it was normal. The box itself felt oddly warm. ... I reached out and touched the metal walls; they were cold to the touch ... (ibid., pp. 11–12)

When Ollendorff took his temperature after he had stepped out of the box, he was surprised to find that it had risen by 2.5 degrees Fahrenheit.

(Wilson was subsequently asked to write an introduction, mentioning Reich, to the British edition of Robert Ollendorff's *Juvenile Homosexual Experience and its Effect on Adult Sexuality* (1974)).

However, the result of all these meetings was

> ... that I was still as far as ever from the "truth about Reich". Was he ... a typical "Outsider", a man driven by a peculiar kind of honesty, an inner vision of truth, which he had to pursue even at the cost of health and sanity? Or was he merely an egotist tormented by a desire for "recognition", by the hunger for self-esteem? (ibid., p. 19)

His book, Wilson explained, was not intended primarily as a biography of Reich:

> As soon as I began to study the available material, I formed the impression that Reich had no intention of allowing anyone to write a frank and fully documented biography. ... He certainly felt that his ideas were more important than his personal history. (ibid., p. 25)

For this reason he chose the title *The Quest for Wilhelm Reich*. He doubted that Reich would have been pleased with his efforts: "But it demonstrates, I think, that he was right about one thing. His ideas *were* more important than his personal history" (ibid., p. 25).

It is not the intention of this essay to summarise the biographical sections of Wilson's book. The most important Chapters are Two and Four which Wilson advises readers to skip if they are only interested in biography. These two chapters outline Wilson's ideas on psychology, and how they relate to Reich's, and it is more appropriate to concentrate on them here.

Chapters Two and Four amount to a full-scale attack on Freud's sexual theory. For Wilson "the conscious mind is as important as the unconscious in the mechanism of neurosis—*precisely* as important, since the two stand in the relation of two tennis players, each playing an equal part in the negative-feedback process" (ibid., p. 127). The results of split-brain research, in the early 1960s, (see *Frankenstein's Castle*: Chapter Four) revealed "that we have two people living inside our heads, one in the left and one in the right hemisphere" (ibid., pp. 122–123). He saw their relationship to be similar to that of Stan Laurel and Oliver (Ollie) Hardy in the old Hollywood films. Ollie, the dominant, bossy type, is the left ("ego") and Stan, the vague and child-like character, the right ("id"). Stan always takes his cues from Ollie. If Ollie is cheerful, Stan is ecstatic; if Ollie is feeling gloomy, Stan becomes depressed. It is Stan, however, who controls the vital energy which he provides in abundance when Ollie is in a positive state of mind. But when Stan becomes depressed, the energy is blocked, Ollie becomes even gloomier, and we find ourselves caught in a downward spiral of negative feedback. This, for Wilson, is the basic mechanism of neurosis, the starting point of which is "not sexual repression, but that initial failure of the right to back up the left" (ibid., p. 127). It is clear to Wilson that "most of Freud's major cases can be interpreted without the sexual theory" (ibid., p. 67) which Freud regarded "with jealous concern, and became deeply resentful and suspicious of anyone who questioned it" (ibid., p. 74). He then goes on to provide alternative explanations for the causes of neurosis in two famous cases: "Little Hans" and "The Wolf Man".

So, was Reich's work based on a fallacy? Wilson's answer was emphatically: "Yes. Reich's work was based on the sexual theory, and the sexual theory is seen to be based on a fallacy ..." (ibid., p. 119). However, Wilson saw an important distinction between Freud and Reich, that of outlook:

> Freud's basic outlook was negative; Reich's was positive. ... For
> Freud, sex was a mere animal instinct whose frustration leads to

neurosis. But why is sex so important to us? Because, says Freud, we are nature's slaves, and nature demands procreation ... For Reich, as for D. H. Lawrence, sex was the most powerful expression of the force of life itself, man's glimpse of reality. That is to say, where sex is concerned, Freud is a rationalist, Reich a mystic. (ibid., p. 119)

But, for Wilson, Reich's notion that neurosis is a form of sexual stasis is not the complete answer: "In fact neurosis *is* a form of stasis—or stagnation. The ego becomes separated from its source of power and energy—just as Reich believed. Reich recognized that the central problem is to start the energy flowing again" (ibid., p. 127).

The right and left brains are like two hikers walking at different speeds: "... if we are to stay mentally healthy, they must be persuaded to walk at the same speed" (ibid., p. 128). This can be done by a variety of methods: meditation, relaxing, becoming "absorbed" in something, listening to music, etc. Sex too *is* a highly effective method of encouraging the two sides of the brain to keep pace with one another: "it causes excitement; but the intensity of pleasure also causes the left to 'slow down' in order to enjoy the experience to the full" (ibid., p. 128). It is indeed, Wilson admits, and as Reich realised, one of the most effective methods of promoting cooperation between the two selves:

> Yet Reich's determined reductionism diluted the value of his insight. His obsession with the sexual impulse prevented him from seeing beyond it; the result is that there is something oddly limited and disappointing about his concept of health. A healthy man or woman is free from sexual stasis. But there is something trivial about this definition. Did Leonardo have to be free from sexual stasis when he painted *The Last Supper*? Or Handel when he composed *The Messiah*? Or Tolstoy when he wrote *War and Peace*? The human spirit is capable of so much more than mere "health". And Reich's psychology has no room for these "higher reaches of human nature". (ibid., pp. 128–129)

In his postscript, Wilson answered the question that many readers would have been asking: why write a book about someone he finds so difficult to like?

> First, because there is a kind of horrifying fascination in watching a man of Reich's immense vitality making a series of wrong

choices that bring him to disaster. But second, and more important, because I feel it impossible to agree with critics who feel that he went off the rails after the discovery of the orgone. (ibid., p. 269)

Unlike those critics, Wilson gave due consideration to the latter half of Reich's career and cautiously provided support for some of his more contentious theories. But for Wilson, the optimist, Reich's psychology left out the most important factor, human freedom: "effective psycho-therapy depends basically upon the will of the patient. ... The psy-chotherapist's most important task is to persuade the patient to start *fighting back*". (ibid., p. 286).

> ... the "unconscious" regions of the mind contain enormous reserves of power ... anyone who accepts the major premise of Freud and Reich—that the unconscious is nothing more than a repository of dangerous repressions—has been robbed of his most powerful weapon against discouragement and defeat. For man is ultimately an evolutionary animal. ... He seems to come closest to fulfilment in *problem-solving*. ... It is as if his deep-est sense of purpose is geared to problem-solving—that is, to creativity ... [and] one of the main reasons he is so obsessed with problem-solving is that when he has successfully over-come some difficult challenge, he receives a strange glimpse of unsuspected powers inside himself. ... It is not even necessary to overcome problems to obtain the same tantalising insight; it can happen on any spring morning or autumn afternoon. (ibid., pp. 286–287)

Wilson's conclusion about Reich was that he was a misunderstood man of genius but "... also a touchy egotist who became his own worst enemy ..." (ibid., p. 19).

* * *

Contemporary reviews of *The Quest for Wilhelm Reich* were mixed. This is best illustrated by contrasting the review by psychiatrist Anthony Storr (1920–2001) with that from the US journal *National Review*; the for-mer, after using eighty-five per cent of the review to give his own views on Reich, praises Wilson for writing "engagingly" but then accuses him of naivety in his assessment of Freud and, in the final analysis, calls the book "silly" (Storr, 1981, p. 43) whilst the latter believes that it provides "… an excellent introduction of the man's ideas and unsettled life" (*National Review*, 1982, p. 782).

CHAPTER SIX

Access to Inner Worlds: The Story of Brad Absetz (1983)

*A*ccess to *Inner Worlds*, a slender but important book in Wilson's canon, was published by Rider & Co. Ltd. in 1983 and reprinted in 1986. It appeared in a Japanese translation by Hirakowa Shuppan-sha (Mind Books) of Tokyo in 1984 but was not published in the US until 1990. An e-book edition of the 1990 text was produced in 2005.

The title of Chapter One: "Beyond left-brain consciousness" refers to the results of split-brain research which was carried out in the US in the early 1960s and became *the* fashionable field in neuroscience. Wilson's discovery of this research, in the mid-1970s, came as something of a revelation to the author whose self-confessed obsession had always been with "the other mode of consciousness". He first mentioned it in the second of his "Occult Trilogy" books, *Mysteries: An Investigation into the Occult, the Paranormal and the Supernatural* (1978). This was followed by a book, specifically about the double brain, entitled *Frankenstein's Castle* (See Chapter Four): "The person you call 'you' lives in the left side of your brain. And a few centimetres away there is another person, a completely independent identity. ... In effect, the left brain is a scientist, the right-brain an artist" (Wilson, 1991, p. 21) (Subsequent research has put into question this notion of the artistic/scientific functions of the two halves of the brain. It will be interesting to see how, or if, this matter is eventually resolved. Wilson, however, insists that "... doubts about the split-brain theory make no difference whatever; the difference between the 'two selves' *does* exist, whether or not they can be closely identified with the left and right" (Wilson, 1986a, p. 99)).

He starts the book with some big questions: What is wrong with human beings? Why do we seem to live in an almost permanent state of unreality? "The basic answer," writes Wilson, "is that human beings are the only creatures who spend 99 per cent of their time *living inside their own heads*" (ibid., p. 13). By this he means: the left cerebral hemisphere. We have developed the world of imagination to help us envisage the future and anticipate any problems that might occur. But this also means that we can create a suffocating prison inside our heads and, as a result, lose contact with the real world. He feels that we need to go beyond left-brain consciousness to access our inner worlds. But a shift too far to the right is not desirable; he advocates that we bring the left and right hemispheres into alignment. When this is achieved we gain a "sudden feeling of reality" (ibid., p. 21):

> The world as seen by left-brain consciousness is flat, two-dimensional, little more than a sketch. The business of the right brain is to add a third dimension. It is this recognition of reality that brings the feeling of relief, the sense that "all is well". ... When the right brain begins to do its proper work, we recognise ... that the world is infinitely richer and more meaningful than the left can grasp. ... And if I can "know" that reality actually has a third dimension, I shall never fall into the mistake of complaining that there is nothing new under the sun and that life is futile. (ibid., p. 21)

But how can we access this "sudden feeling of reality" at will? Wilson proceeds to tell the remarkable story of Brad Absetz who "... stumbled accidentally on the 'trick', and whose life has been transformed by it" (ibid., p. 26).

In the summer of 1981, shortly after a period of intense overwork, Wilson was invited to speak at a ten-day seminar at the Viittakivi Centre in Finland. He was met at Helsinki airport by Absetz, an American, domiciled in Finland, who escorted him by train to the Centre. Wilson describes the scenery *en route* and recounts an important insight:

As we sat in the restaurant car ... I experienced suddenly that curious sense of satisfaction that can only be described in the words "being where you are". That sounds absurd only until we reflect that for most of our lives we are *not* where we are. I am walking down a lane ..., but only my body is there; my mind is "elsewhere". ... And then, beyond a certain point in relaxation, it happens. The left brain slows down; suddenly it is walking in step with the right. And you are there in the present moment, wholly and completely. You can taste the flavour of your own consciousness. (ibid., p. 32)

This is one of those "trademark" personal observations which Wilson has successfully utilised throughout his career to elevate his ideas from the realms of theory into practice. It inspired David Power, in his essay on *Access ...* for the festschrift *Around the Outsider*, to write:

I found that these vivid descriptions of Finland following immediately after the equally vivid descriptions of Wilson's overwork and health issues induced in me—as a reader—that very same sense of being wholly and completely in the present moment. ... I realized that Wilson's books are, in places, as much about inducing ... states of consciousness as being vehicles for talking about them. (Power, 2011, pp. 188–202)

Wilson then casually enquired whether his companion had done any writing. The reply was yes, he had written some poems; Absetz then corrected himself saying that in fact they had "written themselves". Wilson remarked that it sounded as if they were influenced by the right brain and looked forward to reading some of them.

The next day Wilson lectured to the students at the Centre on the "intentionality of consciousness":

... when we see something, we have to reach out and grasp it. ... We imagine that happiness is due to circumstances—holidays, Christmas, unexpected pleasures, and so on. In fact the holiday only stimulates perception, so you can "grasp" twice as hard as usual. The result is that feeling of reality, intensity. If we could deliberately re-programme the unconscious mind to make twice the effort, we could achieve intensity at will. (op. cit., p. 36)

On reflection, later that evening, he felt that the students had been unable to fully grasp his meaning: "They wanted to 'do', not listen" (ibid., p. 37). So the following day he introduced them to the "pen trick" … a basic exercise for inducing deeper intentionality. This involved holding up a pen and concentrating on it to the exclusion of everything else, then relaxing and repeating for ten minutes in combination with a system of "Reichian breathing" (as advocated by the psychologist Wilhelm Reich (1897–1957) about whom Wilson had just written the biographical study *The Quest for Wilhelm Reich* (see Chapter Five)): "The breathing exercise induces deep relaxation and a sense of well-being. The pen exercise induces a sense of control. … The control itself somehow becomes relaxed and confident" (ibid., p. 38). This convinces Wilson that we "can alter our perceptions with an act of will. They are not just something that 'happens to us'" (ibid., p. 37).

Later, Absetz left a notebook of his poetry, or "concentrates" as he called them, in Wilson's room. Wilson read through them and found that his style had a "pleasing simplicity": "What impressed me was that he seldom made the mistake of trying to be literary, or deliberately striking. … Brad's 'concentrates' seemed effortless and sure-footed. They avoided sentimentality as easily as cleverness and display" (ibid., p. 40). Questioning him about how he came to write them revealed "a story so remarkable that I [told] him he ought to write a book about it. He … said he didn't feel he was a writer. And as he talked on, the conviction came upon me that if he wouldn't write the book, then I would do it for him. Before he had finished I even knew what I intended to call it: *Access to Inner Worlds*" (ibid., p. 42).

During periods of intense depression, Absetz's wife would lie on her bed. For hours on end, he would lie beside her, in a relaxed but inwardly alert manner, waiting for her to come out of it. During this time he noticed that his body began to act in a strange way: first his arm would move, seemingly of its own volition, and describe a series of complex "movement-impulses" which affected his whole body and breathing. Later he noticed these "movement-impulses" occurring in his daily life; for example: he would allow his hands to choose foods that he would not normally eat, losing weight and becoming fitter as a result. He also produced poems, drawings, paintings, and metal sculptures in this way. Wilson's reaction to the poems was one of excitement: he considered them to be examples of C. G. Jung's "active imagination" whilst the drawings he found to be Paul Klee-like: "I imagine that Klee was giving expression to the same deep pattern-making impulses of the subconscious" (ibid., p. 55). Wilson observes that this process went in stages: the original movements were aimed at improving Absetz's physical well-being from where the emphasis switched to his mind, with the paintings and sculptures representing a new level of creativity: "Brad's paintings could be regarded as the right-brain demonstrating its freedom from the limitations of the left. It is saying to the left-brain ego: 'I am here. Do not leave me out of account ...'" (ibid., p. 73):

> In those hours of inner suspension, lying beside his wife, simultaneously attentive and relaxed, that 'other self' found its voice could be heard, and that it would no longer be ignored or overruled by the practical ego. Brad had, in fact, taken a vital step towards solving a problem that has preoccupied artists, philosophers and poets for almost two centuries. (ibid., p. 95)

Wilson addresses this problem of "visionary consciousness" in the next chapter, "A century of misunderstanding". Any student coming to Wilson's philosophy for the first time would do well to read this chapter for it contains, succinctly, his essential ideas. "In its most basic form," writes Wilson, this visionary consciousness

> ... is simply a feeling of excitement, of happiness and affirmation. This is accompanied by an insight that seems to be purely objective: that reality is infinitely deeper and richer than it appears to ordinary perception: that, in some paradoxical sense, everyday consciousness is a liar ... (ibid., p. 96)

In European literature, accounts of these moments of visionary consciousness first appeared in the works of the Romantics. The problem that the Romantics encountered, however, was their inability to summon these insights at will, or to sustain them, leading to frustration, self-pity, world-weariness, and defeat. Because we can, like the Romantics, be swept from boredom and frustration one moment to "... experience a momentary immortality, a sense of power, of insight, vision" (ibid., p. 98) the next, Wilson feels that because we "are not swept into these moments on the crest of a wave of ecstasy or vitality ..." they are "only a hair's breadth away from the experience of fatigue and boredom" (ibid., p. 98) and that therefore "life could become a continuous delight if we could learn the trick of looking at things from a slightly different angle" (ibid., p. 99). This leads him to reassert the importance of understanding that perception is intentional:

> ... it is *we* who transform ... the raw material of perception into what we see. Perception is a sculptor, a moulder of reality. ... I fire it like an arrow. If I am feeling bored and passive, then I can scarcely muster the energy to pull back the string, and the arrow falls a few feet away. But if my expected reward ... fills me with desire, I draw the bowstring back as far as it will go, and the arrow thuds into its target. (ibid., p. 107)

This does not mean that we create reality—the meaning is already there—but how much of that reality we experience is very largely down to us. We can enhance our experience by throwing the full weight of our conviction into it or by adopting a sense of optimism assuming that "the world is a delightful place, full of hidden meanings" (ibid., p. 109).

Wilson recounts that when the psychologist Abraham Maslow began talking to his students about "peak experiences", they began to recall peak experiences from the past and the very act of thinking and talking about them induced more: "The peak experience is, in fact, merely 'committed' experience, experience in which the ego exerts full weight, instead of 'hanging back' in the conviction that it is merely a spectator ... *We* cause them by being optimistic and interested" (ibid., p. 113). But we can also cause the opposite to happen: "We allow some dreary prospect to cause a sinking feeling, then accept the sinking feeling as evidence that life is difficult and dangerous—'We can't win'" (ibid., p. 114). "We must grasp this central point," insists Wilson, "that most of our problems are self-inflicted ... *we* choose our reaction to them" (ibid., p. 114). The secret is to know that "you" are the controller of your thoughts and that real thinking involves reason and intuition combined; in other words: "... the close co-operation of both halves of the brain—like two men at either end of a double-handed saw." "And once we have achieved the insight that thought is 'intentional', we can begin to use it to control our perceptions and feelings" (ibid., p. 112).

In the final chapter Wilson gives practical advice on how we can access our inner worlds. He insists that "left-brain consciousness must remain as dominant and powerful as ever, prepared to take over at a moment's notice. Yet it must also be capable of remaining silent; of suspending its dominance to allow the right to develop its own powers of self-expression" (ibid., p. 118). The problem is that in Western man the left brain is hyperactive: "like some enormous factory, it hums and roars with deafening activity" (ibid., p. 118). Wilson suggests a technique to silence the roar:

> Concentrate the mind, as if lifting an enormously heavy weight, and allow the attention to move from part to part of the body, enlisting the cooperation of each part in the collective effort. Clench and unclench the fists; tense and relax the muscles of the arms, the stomach, the thighs. After half a minute or so, relax. Then do it again. (ibid., pp. 119–120)

This has the effect of discharging unused energy and allowing us to relax: "This is an interesting state. For once the protesting voices have been silenced, there is nothing to prevent us from opening the door and walking into the world inside us" (ibid., p. 120). Behind that door is a huge library containing all our memories:

> Even the briefest glimpse of these memories produces a sense of pure delight and astonishment ... because the sheer profusion, the sheer quantity, of these memories seems unnecessary. *Why* has the brain carefully stored up everything that has ever happened to us since birth, if we are never going to make use of it, and if the brain is going to start decomposing within minutes of death? ... There *must* be some other purpose behind human existence, some immense, complex, unfathomable purpose ... (ibid., p. 122)

These memories can then blend together and spread outwards "so that every one evokes half a dozen others, and so on in geometric progression":

> There is a dazzling sensation of hovering above your own life, seeing it as a whole, like some enormous landscape. And as we glimpse these "distant horizons", we also become aware that *this* is what memory is *for*. Not fragmentary, piecemeal perceptions, but a total grasp. And not only of my own life, but, by some process of deduction, of other lives, of all life. (ibid., p. 122)

Wilson believes that the existence of this library proves that man was intended to have "a deeper, more vivid type of consciousness" (ibid., p. 124) and if we are to achieve this we must, first of all, know that the library is there and start using it. In order to do this we "have to learn deep relaxation, learn to still the left brain and senses" (ibid., p. 124). This enables the right brain to supply the third-dimension to the two-dimensional left-brain experience; when reading, for example, Shelley's "Ode to the West Wind", the "inner librarian" might create the roaring wind in the trees and the smell of autumn leaves. Or when reading a book about the history of London, the "inner librarian" can recreate your last visit: the smell of the underground, the breeze in the tunnel as the train approaches, the sound of the doors opening:

> This ability to "real-ise" another time and place, I call Faculty X. It is quite clearly a natural ability we all possess. … Only now … are we beginning to recognise that such states are within our control; not only that, but that they offer the promise of the most fascinating step in human evolution so far. (ibid., p. 134)

The importance of enlisting the help of the "other self" is re-emphasised by Wilson and here, near the end of the book, he reveals a useful method of enabling us to do just that. The answer was provided by Brad Absetz who insisted that the "other self" is perfectly willing to help if we are willing to listen:

> "Listening" must here be understood as an active suspension of our automatic functions, an attitude of vigilance, of alertness. Most of us waste about 90 per cent of our lives in purely automatic living. In order to suspend this, I merely have to behave as if I am listening intently for some important noise, like the ringing of a telephone. And as I remain in this condition of "openness", my vital powers begin to rise in me, like water in a well. (ibid., p. 137)

He concludes: "The crucial step in individual evolution is quite simply to recognise the existence of that 'other self'. When this happens we are ready to embark upon the most interesting experiment of all: to discover what our two selves can do when they enter into active collaboration" (ibid., p. 135).

* * *

The book, unfortunately, received few reviews, almost certainly because, although essentially a book about psychology, it was published by the renowned esoteric publishers Rider & Co. Howard F. Dossor, however, in 1990, saw it as a "profoundly important work" and went on to write: "Many regard it as Wilson's most important book of the past ten years. Certainly it made it clear that there were positive connections between his writings on the occult, and those on human psychology and the new existentialism" (Dossor, 1990, pp. 112 & 36). David Power, in his afore-mentioned essay, considers it to be "a neglected gem in Wilson's overall output" (Power, 2011, p. 202).

Wilson had been accused in the past of heralding a new dawn in human evolution but not providing any practical clues as to how that was to be achieved. *Access to Inner Worlds*, a brief but important work, laid that criticism to rest.

CHAPTER SEVEN

Lord of the Underworld: Jung and the Twentieth Century (1984/1988)

Wilson's short study of Carl Gustav Jung (1865–1961) was first published on 26 April 1984 by the Aquarian Press in the UK. It was reprinted in 1988 under the title *C. G. Jung: Lord of the Underworld* and appeared that year in the US. French, Finnish, German, Dutch, and Swedish editions, among others, have also, at various times, been available. It was the second in a series of short, largely biographical, studies written by Wilson for Aquarian on important non-mainstream thinkers: *The War Against Sleep: The Philosophy of Gurdjieff* had appeared in 1980 and studies of Rudolf Steiner (1861–1925), Aleister Crowley (1875–1947), and P. D. Ouspensky (1878–1947) followed in 1985, 1987, and 1993 respectively.

The first six chapters give a brief account of Jung's early life, his interest in the occult, his early career as Freud's principal disciple, his break with Freud, and summarises the key concepts of "archetypes", "the collective unconscious", "synchronicity", "individuation", and "active imagination". Wilson, whilst acknowledging Jung's "remarkable body of work that can bear comparison with the oeuvre of any of the major figures of the nineteenth century" (Wilson, 1988, p. 124) did, however, have a number of reservations, which he revealed in flashes throughout the early chapters but brought together in Chapter Seven, "Doubts and reservations". He was clearly annoyed by Jung's early obsession "with sounding like a paid-up member of the scientific establishment", the result being "a kind of rigidity in his mental categories, a lack of perceptiveness" (ibid., p. 39).

But whereas many critics found fault with Jung's preoccupation with the occult, Wilson had "... no quarrel whatever with Jung's occultism, since it was all based on personal experience ..." (ibid., p. 124). In his introduction, Wilson recounted Jung's near-death experience when he was sixty-eight years old. This caused a "... profound change in his outlook [and] seems to have made him less defensive about presenting his deepest convictions, less concerned about being accused of stepping beyond the limits of science" (ibid., p. 8).

Wilson realised, however, probably from his own experience, that "... one of the main difficulties of the world of the paranormal is that once an investigator has expressed cautious acceptance of any one aspect of it, he finds it almost impossible to stay within his chosen limits" (ibid., p. 16).

Jung's concept of "synchronicity" "implies that 'powers' outside us are organising coincidences to draw our attention to new facts, or that the unconscious mind itself can somehow influence matter" (ibid., p. 16). This was a concept of particular importance to Wilson who wrote at length on it in several later books, none more so than the essay on his "Outsider Cycle" for my *Colin Wilson's Outsider Cycle: A Guide for Students* (2009):

> It is my own experience that coincidences like this seem to happen when I am in "good form"—when I am feeling alert, cheerful and optimistic, and not when I am feeling tired, bored or gloomy ... We are all at our best when the imagination is awake, and we can sense the presence of that "other self", the intuitive part of us. (Wilson, 2009, p. 145)

So "... when we are psychologically healthy, synchronicities should occur all the time" (op. cit., p. 154).

He did, however, "... feel dubious about some of [Jung's] purely psychological theories" (ibid., p. 124), in particular the concepts of "archetypes" and "the collective unconscious" which he saw as a kind of underworld below Freud's "unconscious". He accused Jung of having an "unnecessarily complicated" approach to the treatment of some of his patients who, as a result, were not altogether cured:

> In fact, if psychology means understanding the *mechanisms* of the mind ... then Jung was not a particularly good psychologist. With his eyes fixed on his sonar gauges, looking for signs of what goes on in the black depths, he overlooks more straightforward mechanisms of neurosis. (ibid., p. 131)

Wilson was much more comfortable with Pierre Janet's (1859–1947) explanation of neurosis as being caused by a "lowering of the mind threshold" (ibid., p. 127). "Mental health depends upon the sense of reality, a constant 'feedback' between the mind and the environment" (ibid., p. 132). Wilson felt that our "robot" (that part of our mind that does learned tasks automatically), can undermine our "reality function", causing tiredness, boredom, even "life failure": "Modern man is constantly slipping into this state of non-interaction, which results in a drop in energy. This in turn makes him feel that 'nothing is worth the effort' ..." (ibid., p. 132). "Neurosis," asserted Wilson, "is a damaged will to live. Psychosis is the mind's attempt to compensate for the damaged will to live by providing an 'alternative reality'" (ibid., p. 132).

Wilson considered Jung's concept of "active imagination" to be "one of the most interesting and exciting of all Jung's ideas" (ibid., p. 145) and devoted a ten-page "Appendix" to it. He also considered this appendix important enough to be included in the self-edited *The Essential Colin Wilson* (1985).

In 1913, when Jung was under severe stress, he decided to "let-go" and allow the image-making powers of the subjective mind to flood into consciousness:

> He called the result "active imagination", but we can see that it was not imagination in the ordinary sense of the word: the deliberate evocation of mental images or states. What Jung had achieved was a *new balance* between the ego and the unconscious, in which the unconscious was recognised as an equal partner. (ibid., p. 148)

Following his discovery of the results of split-brain research in the mid-1970s (see *Frankenstein's Castle*: Chapter Four) Wilson had emphasised the importance of this *new balance* between the left and the right sides of the brain. In one of his renowned analogies he compared the relationship of the ego (left brain) and the unconscious (right brain) to that of a great conductor and his orchestra:

> ... the orchestra that has come to respond to his most delicate gesture. But such a state of harmony depends on the initial recognition that *I* am the conductor ... The greatest danger of "active imagination" is that the subject should assume it means handing over the baton to the orchestra ... Active imagination is a state of cooperation in which the ego must remain the dominant partner. (ibid., p. 155)

He saw Western man as a conductor who is unaware that he possesses an orchestra "or is only dimly and intermittently aware of it. Active imagination is a technique of becoming aware of the orchestra. This is 'individuation'" (ibid., p. 155). But this is also only a beginning: "The next task is to develop a random collection of musicians into a great orchestra."

* * *

There were no substantial contemporary reviews of this book but a number have subsequently appeared on the internet. Professor Bruce Charlton described it as a "... marvellously insightful short study ..." (Charlton, 2015). Bobby Maltherne, however, wrote: "The safest judgement on Wilson's biographical work is that they tell us a great deal about Wilson and his basic ideas; how much they tell us about Jung must remain an open question" (Maltherne, 2004). Donald Scott on *Goodreads* thought: "For those interested in finding out more about one of the key thinkers in psychotherapy, I can recommend this thin paperback ..." (Scott, 2014).

There is something to be said for a combination of all three of these reviews. In my short assessment in *The Ultimate Colin Wilson Bibliography*, I wrote:

> A very personal assessment of Jung which inevitably sheds as much light on Wilson as it does on Jung. Particularly interesting

are the last two chapters, in which Wilson states his doubts and reservations about aspects of Jung's work, while still highlighting what he considers to be the psychiatrist's major achievements. (Stanley, 2015, p. 142)

CHAPTER EIGHT

The Misfits: A Study of Sexual Outsiders (1988)

*T*he *Misfits*, arguably Colin Wilson's most controversial book, was published in February 1988 by Grafton Books in the UK and Carroll & Graf, a year later, in the US, with Spanish and Japanese translations following. Even the choice of cover courted controversy, the UK edition sporting a reproduction of the painting "Maid to Order III" by Allen Jones (1937-) which was banned in Scotland and not used for the US edition.

It was Wilson's third non-fiction book specifically about sexuality: he had published, in 1963, as volume five of his "Outsider Cycle", *Origins of the Sexual Impulse* (see Chapter Two) and, in 1966, *Sex and the Intelligent Teenager*. The latter was written as a response to a book by Barbara Cartland (1901–2000): *Sex and the Teenager* (1964) which purported to give advice to young people on sexual behaviour but instead contained sentences like: "I can assure you that decently brought up boys don't think much of girls who allow real kissing the first evening they go out together" (quoted in Wilson, 1966, p. 17). Wilson's response was (and it should be noted that this was 1966—the eve of the so-called "sexual revolution"): "... it is time that everybody learned to think intelligently about sex. No subject is more surrounded by stupidity and lies. ... My chief aim is to get you to engage in the unfashionable exercise of thinking, which most of your elders and betters gave up a long time ago" (ibid., pp. 17 & 19).

Wilson certainly thought deeply about human sexuality; it permeated his work, both fiction and non-fiction, and so, in some ways, it is surprising that it took him so long, after his famous first book *The Outsider* (1956), to write a book specifically about *sexual* outsiders. But it wasn't until 1971 that he first met with the remarkable Dr. Charlotte Bach (1920–1981), whose life story and ideas form the basis of *The Misfits*.

Bach wrote to Wilson, after reading *Origins of the Sexual Impulse*, enclosing sections of a work in progress (still unpublished) entitled *Homo Mutans, Homo Luminens*. Wilson, despite finding her style somewhat convoluted, stuck with it and was sufficiently intrigued to meet up with her in London: "She proved to be a broad-shouldered mammoth of a woman with a deep masculine voice and a heavy Hungarian accent" (Wilson, 1988, p. 21). He suspected that her interest in sexual perversion was not altogether academic, as she asserted. In 1973, *Time Out* asked Wilson to write an article about her: "One of the greatest intellectual advances of the twentieth century: an evaluation of the work of Charlotte Bach" (no. 164, 13–19 April 1973, pp. 13–15). He then outlined her theories in a chapter entitled "Evolution" in the second volume of his "Occult Trilogy": *Mysteries: An Investigation into the Occult, the Paranormal and the Supernatural* (1978).

> As far as I could make out, her basic idea was this. There is in every man and woman a powerful element of the opposite sex, which attracts like a magnet. In other words, every male has a deep unconscious desire to *become* a woman, and every female has the same urge to become a man. This makes us sexually unstable and explains why there are so many sexual perversions. But it is precisely this instability that makes human beings so creative and has led to the amazing growth of human culture and civilisation. Culture is not simply the outcome of man's craving for security and happiness; it is the outcome of his "sickness". (ibid., p. 20)

Bearing this in mind, it seemed highly appropriate (but still a shock to those, like Wilson, who knew her) that when Charlotte Bach died in 1981 it was discovered that she was, in fact, a man: Karoly Hajdu!

In the light of this startling discovery, Wilson wrote "The real Charlotte", for *Encounter* (volume 59, nos. 3–4, Sept/Oct 1982, pp. 9–18) and "Charlotte Bach", for *Time Out* (April 13–19, 1983, pp. 13–15), following this up with an article in the *Hampstead and Highgate Express*: "Charlotte's strange evolution" (25 October 1985, p. 81). In *The Misfits* the opening two chapters are spent discussing her theory of evolution, which he finally rejects. The next chapter deals with the Marquis de Sade (1740–1814) whose views on sexual perversion: "... amounts to a flat contradiction of Charlotte Bach's theory ..." (ibid., p. 46):

> If perversion were really due to our innate male-female polarity, then it would have been the same down the ages [but] what we would now label perversion is largely a product of the nineteenth century, and the factor behind its emergence is not transsexuality but a strange morbid flowering of the imagination. (ibid., p. 70)

Wilson's views on the impact of what he calls the first imaginative novels (i.e., Samuel Richardson's *Pamela* (1740) and *Clarissa* (1748) and Jean-Jacques Rousseau's *Julie, or the New Heloise* (1761); novels that "taught Europe to dream ..." (ibid., p. 78)), discussed at length in his *The Craft of the Novel* (1975), are reiterated in the chapter "Romantic agonies":

> The invention of the novel was one of the greatest steps in the evolution of human imagination. ... It was inevitable that someone should use the new invention to amplify sexual emotions, and to create the literary *genre* we call pornography. (ibid., p. 91)

In the next chapter, "Rebel angel", Wilson points out how Byron, De Sade, and others "needed the smell of 'forbiddenness' to enjoy sex" (ibid., p. 113), to make them feel more "alive", to stimulate what he calls the "reality function". This, according to Wilson, is a mistake perpetuated by all libertines: "... before we can feel really alive, the mind needs to add a dimension of reality to the world of the senses. ... Our greatest problem is that our reality function is so feeble [it] needs to be constantly stimulated ..." (ibid., p. 112). The key to breaking free from this loop is to realise that the reality function needs to be stimulated from inside rather than outside. Wilson asserts that if we could learn to develop a more powerful and efficient reality function "then life would seem to become a perpetual delight" (ibid., p. 112).

The following chapter attempts to show how the "imagination revolution" developed a darker side, which led to the rise of sexual crime. He concludes, however, that although it would not be totally accurate to suggest that there was some connection between the rise of pornography and sex crime:

> All the same, we can feel clearly that sex crime was the end-product of a process that had begun with Richardson and Cleland. A *state of mind* had gradually spread until, to some extent, it affected every level of society. By the second half of the nineteenth century, imagination—which had seemed so harmless in *Pamela*—was suddenly revealing its darker and more disquieting aspects. (ibid., pp. 141–142)

In the ensuing chapter, "Victorian misfits", Wilson reveals how pornographers like "Walter", the author of *My Secret Life* (c.1888) used the lure of the "forbidden" to produce "... 'superheated sex', as Victorian engineers learned the trick of producing superheated steam" (ibid., p. 137). However, being a "gentlemen", who had been taught to express himself, he saved his "brutality for the realm of language" (ibid., p. 169). Wilson felt that it was inevitable that "those who were less fortunate should be tempted to cross the gap that divides sexual fantasy from sex crime" (ibid., p. 169). He sees the Jack the Ripper murders of 1888 (about which Wilson is an acknowledged expert) as "a kind of watershed between the century of Victorian values and the age of violence that was to come" (ibid., p. 171).

Chapter Eight, "Guilt and defiance", starts with a mild version of Wilson's criticism of Freud's sexual theory and progresses to a discussion of the life and work of Havelock Ellis (1859–1939), Richard von Krafft-Ebing (1840–1902), Magnus Hirschfeld (1868–1935), and others. Then he turns his attention to those dramatists and novelists of the early twentieth century who contributed to the "sexual revolution": Marcel Proust (1871–1922), James Joyce (1882–1941), D. H. Lawrence (1885–1930), and Henry Miller (1891–1980). But Wilson finds their romantic idea of freedom unpalatable: "They all insist that man has no responsibility except to himself, and that the only part of himself that he needs to cultivate is his intuition. Because they distrust the intellect, they are forced to base their visionary philosophy on intuition." But, insists Wilson, it is impossible to build a philosophy without the support of the intellect: "Their refusal to have any truck with intellect leaves them all in a hopelessly contradictory position—hence the pessimism and despair." If we can avoid this "the prospect begins to look altogether more promising" (ibid., p. 201).

In the final chapter, "Misfits or mystics?", Wilson discusses the sadism of Percy Grainger (1882–1961) and John Cowper Powys (1872–1963), James Joyce's masochism and D. H. Lawrence's "preference for sodomy" (ibid., p. 212), concluding that all sexual aberrations are "an attempt to achieve a higher level of vitality" (ibid., p. 206). He argues that these men have "learned to intensify consciousness through the use of sexual imagination" (ibid., p. 212). There is, says Wilson, "an aspect of oneself that can be made to respond to sexual imaginings just as another aspect might respond to music or poetry" (ibid., p. 212). This he sees as the "sexual illusion" which "depends on a *deliberately cultivated* self-division: a division between a 'childish' and a 'grown-up' aspect of the personality" (ibid., p. 213):

> ... cultivating "the hidden child" can be a dangerous game. The whole point about growing up is that we develop an increased *control*—over ourselves and the world around us. The more we achieve this control, the more we become "individuals" instead of helpless bundles of fears and anxieties. This is why Jung calls the process "individuation". The man who cultivates his sexual deviations ... is resisting the process of individuation. He prefers to remain self-divided because, as William Blake said: "stolen joys are sweet, and bread eaten in secret pleasant".
> (ibid., p. 213)

Ironically Jung himself is seen as an example of this, as is Bertrand Russell (1872–1970) and Paul Tillich (1886–1965). Two "Outsiders"—T. E. Lawrence (1888–1935) and Ludwig Wittgenstein (1889–1951)—who Wilson first wrote about at length in *The Outsider* (1956) and *Religion and the Rebel* (1957), were, however, "both driven by an immense dissatisfaction with themselves":

> And behind this lies the greatest and most irritating problem of human existence: the fact that, when confronted by crisis, we suddenly understand the meaning of freedom, and then grasp how *easy* it would be to live on a more intense level of vitality and

purpose. Yet almost as soon as the crisis vanishes, we sink back
into the "triviality of everydayness" (Heidegger's phrase), and find
ourselves totally unable to galvanise ourselves back into a state of
purpose. (ibid., pp. 228–229)

In the postscript, "The fifth window", Wilson returns to *his* theory of
the imaginative revolution, which he feels "provides a basic mechanism for evolution" (ibid., p. 253). The sexual "misfits" previously
discussed made "the mistake of thinking that the key to [higher states
of consciousness] lay in the sexual urge". But, argues Wilson, "[T]he
sexual urge derives its strength from the body and the emotions, and
is not powerful enough to lift us to a new level of conscious awareness. This can be achieved only with the aid of the intellect" (ibid., p.
253). To those who argue that, in a largely illiterate Europe, Wilson's
theory is unlikely, he counters by suggesting that the imaginative revolution could possibly have reached every level of society by the process
that Sir Julian Huxley (1887–1975) called "cultural osmosis" or, more
likely, in his opinion, by "morphic resonance" as proposed by Rupert
Sheldrake (1942-).

Ever the optimist, Wilson thinks that we have reached what he calls
"the feedback point" in the history of consciousness: "the feedback
point is that stage at which the pleasure—or profit—from any activity
is greater than the effort we put into it":

> Life has so far been forced to evolve through pain and inconven-
> ience. … Yet, in the past few thousand years, man has begun to
> realise that the pursuit of knowledge can be enjoyed for its own
> sake, and that knowledge brings him a new sense of control, so
> that being alive becomes a pleasure in itself. He can still be under-
> mined by fatigue or discouragement; yet in his moments of insight,
> he recognises that these miseries are largely self-inflicted … they
> are subjective rather than objective. The moment we clearly recog-
> nise this, we have come close to the feedback point at which we
> would become "undiscourageable". A study of the history of the
> past few centuries suggests that we are now close to the feedback
> point in the history of consciousness—that man is on the point of
> achieving full consciousness of his evolutionary purpose. (ibid.,
> pp. 261–262)

To bring this about we need to learn how to develop our "hidden powers", chiefly the function he has labelled "Faculty X": "the ability to suddenly *grasp* the reality of other times and places" (ibid., p. 260). In his classic study *The Occult* Wilson insisted that "Faculty X" is "the key not only to so-called occult experience, but to the whole future evolution of the human race" (Wilson, 1973b, p. 77).

* * *

The critical response was largely negative although it would be fair to say that *The Misfits* got the critics into something of a tangle and consequently brought out the worst in them. For example: Peter Fuller in *The Guardian*, called it an "unbelievably stupid book" (Fuller, 1988, p. 24); Tim Clark, clearly in frustration, entitled his review for *Time Out* (no. 911, February 3–10, 1988) "For fuck's sake!"; David Profumo, equally unprofessionally, wrote: "It could just be me, but I found it almost impossible to make head or tail of the latest volume by the ubiquitous Colin Wilson" (Profumo, 1988, pp. 26–28). Scott Bradfield couldn't seem to make up his mind one way or the other: "Wilson is incredibly casual and irresponsible as he flings around his grandiose assertions about X-factors [sic] and penises, but there remains nevertheless a certain mesmerizing quality about his smorgasbord of literary references and facile philosophical quotations, which probably shouldn't be taken very seriously, but which might not be worth ignoring altogether" (Bradfield, 1989, p. 29). Wilson was even lampooned in *Private Eye*, an article which included a cartoon of him in a dress! ("Outside loon", *Private Eye*, no. 683, 19 February 1988, p. 24). It was down to Roger Baker to write a serious assessment: "This exploration of pornography and sex crimes does contain quite a lot of interesting ideas and offers some unusual perspectives on sexual behaviour." However, he has reservations: "… there are many levels (historical, literary and even medical) on which this work could be contested. I don't see this as a bad thing. I like provocative books and this one has certainly sent me chasing up all kinds of interesting references." Baker's chief concern is that the book concentrated overmuch on male sexuality: "in any discourse on pornography, sex crime and fetishism the position and attitudes of women must be addressed … this … seems to me a striking omission in what, despite its many irritations, is a stimulating book" (Baker, 1988, pp. 40–42).

In the US it received a positive review: "A wonderfully smooth writer, Wilson challenges and engages in this radical reassessment of sexuality that some will … hopefully, recognise as yet another noteworthy … casting of thought by one of the more visionary writers of our time" (*Kirkus Reviews*, 1988, p. 1596).

In one of the few positive UK reviews, Anthony Burgess (1917–1993), in *The Observer*, observed: "Like all his work, it is vigorous, vulnerable, and breathes the bracing ozone of autodidactism" (Burgess, 1988, p. 52), which provoked the following response from Howard F. Dossor:

> Some part of the negative criticism addressed at Wilson can be explained in terms of a single word that appeared again and again in criticisms of his early books. Wilson, so we were told, was an *autodidact* [which] means simply "self-taught" but the use of the term in relation to Wilson has … a somewhat skewed meaning. … There is … a resistance to Wilson's thinking that may be based on a rejection of the idea that the individual is capable of taking responsibility for his own personal development—both intellectual and emotional. … The myth that learning is the product of teaching is [thereby] preserved. … The autodidact comprehends that there is no teaching where there is no learning. It is a lesson that our universities might well assimilate. (Dossor, 1990, pp. 288–290)

CHAPTER NINE

Super Consciousness: The Quest for the Peak Experience (2007/2009)

W hen Colin Wilson died in December 2013, it was suggested by one obituary writer that, despite the seemingly diverse subject matter of his books, his legacy lay in the field of consciousness studies. This is undoubtedly true and in *Super Consciousness* Wilson, nearing the end of his creative life, decided to summarise his major ideas. Although first published in Japanese in 2007 as *The Search for Power Consciousness*, it was conceived twelve years earlier when the book "... took shape in 48 hours in the form of a 60-page outline ..." (Wilson, 2009a, p. 6). For various reasons it was set aside although the outline was published in 2002 as part of the double e-book *The Ladder of Selves and The Search for Power Consciousness* with an introduction by Wilson scholar Chris Nelson. The full version was first published in English by Watkins Publishing in 2009, as a printed book and an e-book simultaneously.

In the foreword Wilson states: "I am now 75, and most of my life has been devoted to a search for what might be called 'the mechanisms of the Peak Experience', or 'power consciousness' This book might be regarded as a kind of DIY manual of how to achieve it" (ibid., p. 1). "Peak Experience" "(... the experience of sudden overwhelming happiness, the feeling that life is wonderful ..." (ibid., p. 3)) was a concept coined by the American psychologist Abraham Maslow who had written to Wilson in the early 1960s after reading *The Age of Defeat* (1959) (see Chapter One). Finding common ground, they met on several occasions, and corresponded over a number of years, until Maslow's death. Wilson was asked to write a book about him in 1969 and, to this end, Maslow sent him several hours of tape-recorded material about himself and his work. This was published in 1972 as *New Pathways in Psychology: Maslow and the Post-Freudian Revolution* (see Chapter Three). Maslow believed that "peak experiences" just came and went and could not be induced; Wilson thought otherwise.

He argues that "[m]en are only truly happy and free when they are in duo-consciousness" (ibid., p. 17). Duo-consciousness is the experience of being in two places at once: the comfort we feel when we hear the rain beating on the window, for example, and we are sitting relaxing by the fire. It was the Romantics who first discovered that "... they possessed an outer being and an inner being ..." (ibid., p. 15) and that when we relax we can discover it too. The problem with the Romantics was that they did not feel that they belonged in this boring, practical world and found it difficult to adjust to ordinary life after experiencing visions of ecstasy and romance. Many killed themselves or died young heralding the "tragic generation" of the 1890s and the twentieth century: the age of defeat.

Wilson points out that "[b]oredom and lack of purpose are among the most destructive states we can experience" (ibid., p. 25). He emphasises the importance of acknowledging the reality of free will, asserting that once this is realised it encourages an optimism that can make "... the difference between mental health and sickness" (ibid., p. 24). He encourages us to seek out something that will absorb our attention because this has the "automatic effect of focusing our energy" (ibid., p. 26). For many of us sex can do this; Wilson sees sex as an effective means of producing "flow" or "peak experiences":

> Flow is the opposite of stagnation and boredom. William James speaks of a football player who plays the game *technically* perfectly; and then one day, he is taken over by the excitement of the play, and suddenly *the game is playing him*. This is the essence of the flow experience. It is evolution in action: we can *feel* ourselves evolving. (ibid., pp. 32–33)

But essentially, for Wilson, the full significance of sex "… lies in its imaginative dimension":

> … sexual fantasy can achieve such extraordinary intensity because it can call upon the energies of the unconscious mind, and that the next step in human evolution will enable us to bring the same intensity to *all* fantasy … (ibid., p. 30)

A later chapter, "Faculty X and the sexual vision", expands upon this. "Faculty X" is a term that Wilson uses "to pin down the odd ability to grasp the reality of some other time and place. It is basically 'duo-consciousness', being in two places at once" (ibid., p. 147). Wilson suggests that we can generate "Faculty X" through the deliberate exercise of imagination: "… not imagination in the usual sense of mere fantasy, but in Blake's sense of conjuring up another reality" (ibid., p. 149).

In Chapter Four, Wilson turns his attention to cosmic consciousness and provides several examples of writers, poets, and philosophers who have achieved intense mystical experiences:

> What I learned from mystics and poets was that "everyday consciousness" is only one of the many possible states, and that we become trapped in it by assuming that it is the only kind. But Maslow's students discovered that all that was necessary to achieve the states he called peak experiences was to talk about them and think about them until you have reminded yourself how close they are to our normal state. (ibid., p. 51)

In Chapter Five, "The near and the far", Wilson provides his potted history of Romanticism and explains how, in the twentieth century, existentialism became "Romanticism Mark Two". He then proceeds to outline his own position:

> Philosophically speaking, I have devoted all my writing life to trying to create what might be called "Romanticism Mark Three"—a positive existentialism, that declines to accept this "premise of meaninglessness" that is found in Sartre, Camus, Foucault, Derrida and other fashionable thinkers of the past 50 years. This "new existentialism", based upon the phenomenological method of Edmund

Husserl, is the intellectual foundation of my own "non-pessimistic existentialism". (ibid., p. 79)

Wilson launches a full-scale attack on pessimism in Chapter Six, "The paradoxes of nihilism":

If you go into an art gallery that is badly lit, you can't see the pictures properly. Yet you don't declare that they are therefore bad pictures. That is what the pessimistic philosopher is asserting about life. (ibid., p. 84)

According to Wilson consciousness is *intentional* and we need to learn to fire our attention at the world to see it as it is. In order to achieve this a certain cleansing of the doors of perception is necessary: "The moral is that before you try to see in the dark you must make sure that the torch batteries are charged" (ibid., p. 110).

Wilson's *bête noire* Samuel Beckett (1906–1989) bears the brunt of his attack:

One thing is clear. Beckett is saying that our world is not just indifferent to human beings. It is actively malicious. Which would seem to imply that he is not an objective observer, but is getting his emotions—and self-pity—involved. In other words, he cannot be regarded as trustworthy." (ibid., p. 106)

To say that ... his works did no harm would be an evasion. To kill hope *is* to do harm. *The Unnamable* and *Endgame* were conceived out of despair, and their aim is to make others share it. (ibid., p. 109)

In Chapter Eight, Wilson delves into split-brain physiology to provide a clue as to how we can "charge our batteries". He asserts that we have, in effect, two brains and that the person you call "you" lives in the left side of your brain. A few centimetres away, in the right side of the brain, there is another person. The business of the left is to "cope" with everyday problems whilst the business of the right is to deal with our inner-states and feelings: "In short you could say that the left is a scientist, and the right is an artist" (ibid., p. 116).

Wilson had already written a book about this: *Frankenstein's Castle: The Right Brain: Door to Wisdom* in 1980 (see Chapter Four). As already established, he correlates the two brains with Stan Laurel and Oliver Hardy from the Hollywood films: Ollie, the dominant, bossy type, is the left and Stan, the vague and childlike character, the right. The secret is to get Stan and Ollie to work together in a positive way: when we are tired we only need to become absorbed in something to feel the energy and optimism come flowing back. And: "As soon as we experience an optimistic state of mind, Stan and Ollie begin to demonstrate what they can do ..." (ibid., p. 123) producing a rising happiness, which raises our optimism "... which in turn causes another flood of happiness, which reinforces the optimism ..." (ibid., p. 123): a truly "positive feedback".

> This ... also explains why Maslow's students kept on having peak experiences once they began talking about them to one another. Clearly, this is an insight of staggering importance. Armed with this, we are already halfway to achieving PEs at will. (ibid., p. 124)

Wilson turns his attention to synchronicity in Chapter Ten, "Strange powers": "... preposterous coincidences give us a strong sense that what we assume to be 'reality' is really some kind of deception" (ibid., p. 139). He notices that an optimistic state of mind induces synchronicities and goes on to give some extra-ordinary examples from his own experience and from that of others. He concludes:

> ... the implication of synchronicity would seem to be that when we are in spiritual health ... with a high level of vital purpose ... synchronicities tend to favour us. This also implies clearly that gloom and depression are dangerous states of mind. ... In *The Outsider* I suggested that ... if you cease to make all effort, fate takes advantage of this lowering of your spiritual guard by hitting you on the head ... (ibid., p. 145)

Integral to this, according to Wilson, is our acknowledgment of free will. He claims that we live too much of our life "robotically" (i.e., under the influence of what he terms "the robot": that part of our brain that does mundane tasks for us but which we allow to take over more pleasurable activities too): "... we only have to make an effort to raise our vitality by one degree, so we are 49 per cent robot and 51 per cent 'real you', to recognise that freedom is a reality" (ibid., p. 145). In his critique of philosophy (Chapter Twelve) he writes:

> Philosophers have always aimed at some "system" that explains everything. We have to grasp that this is a mirage because—as Kierkegaard said—it leaves me *and my free will* out of account. (ibid., p. 179)

This chapter reiterates "The strange story of modern philosophy" in his 1965 book—the last in his "Outsider Cycle"—*Beyond the Outsider*. He argues that:

> ... real philosophy demands an active attitude, rather than the passive one of the philosopher sitting in his armchair. To "know" something merely with the mind is hardly to know it at all. Our whole being is somehow involved in true knowing. And when this happens, knowledge has a "weight" that is not found in merely intellectual knowing. (ibid., p. 170)

He considers Edmund Husserl to be "... the greatest of modern think-ers" (ibid., p. 169):

> Husserl's basic recognition is that *perception is intentional*; that when we "see" something we fire our attention at it like an arrow. But if there is an "intentional arrow", there must also be an archer who shoots it ... a "real me" (transcendental ego) behind perception ... (ibid., p. 170)

To understand this is to grasp the key to "super" or "power" consciousness:

> Rupert Brooke said that on a spring morning he sometimes walked down a country road feeling almost sick with excitement.
> Brooke realized that he could bring on this feeling by looking at things in a certain way. And what was really happening when he did this was that he had somehow become aware that he could see more, become aware of more, by looking at things as if they pos-sessed hidden depths of meaning. For it is true. He was becoming conscious of the intentional element in perception, that his "seeing" was in itself a creative act. (ibid., p. 173)

In the final chapter, "Achieving power consciousness", Wilson reveals that he has taught himself "the basic method of achieving 'power consciousness'—that is how to go about summoning it at will" (ibid., p. 180). He describes how he had to concentrate intensely for over two hours when driving through snow. Finally, when able to relax:

> I noticed that everything I looked at seemed curiously real and interesting. The ... concentrated attention had somehow "fixed" my consciousness in a higher state of awareness. There was also an immense feeling of optimism. ... My perception seemed clearer, as if I had put on a new and more powerful pair of spectacles. (ibid., p. 181)

He emphasises that "... if you wish to reinforce an insight so it can never fade, you must put twice as much energy into the learning process" (ibid., p. 204). The concentration necessary to stop the car from sliding into a ditch served to push his consciousness beyond its normal mechanical level. He then delineates the "seven levels of consciousness" available to us (see my essay on Wilson's *Beyond the Occult* in *Colin Wilson's "Occult Trilogy": A Guide for Students* (2013) for more details of this). Level four is normal consciousness and when we move towards its upper level "[a]n odd feeling of inner strength begins to arise. ... At its upper end, Level 4 is close to 'power consciousness' ..." (ibid., p. 205). It is here that we sometimes slip into the "peak experience" that Wilson sees as the spark that leaps the gap between levels four and five, "spring morning consciousness": "... when the whole world is self-evidently fascinating and delightful ..." (ibid., p. 205). This can be made permanent on attaining level six: "As for the human race, this would be the decisive step to becoming something closer to gods" (ibid., p. 208).

* * *

In his review of *Super Consciousness* Geoff Ward wrote:

> Wilson has written extensively about the paranormal, the effects of which he is sure are linked to the mind's untapped potential, and one finds the essence of his work in the fusion of its two major strands, existentialism and occultism. He is one of the few thinkers who has stood out against the endemic pessimism and defeatism of our times, and the tendency to reject substance

and meaning in favour of image and ephemera. (Ward, 2009, p. 22)

And in his essay for the festschrift *Around the Outsider* he adds: "Like all great philosophers and artists ... Wilson expands our moral imagination, and the idea that our evolving consciousness fosters the good is implicit in his critique" (Ward, 2011, p. 224).

Mike King asks: "What has over a half-century of reflection on the problem of intensity he so brilliantly dissected in *The Outsider* led to in his new work?"

He has clearly followed all the key intellectual developments during this time, and has interesting observations to make on Phenomenology and the thought of Derrida for example. ... [He] lies outside of the academy, involves "big-picture" thinking, and is capable of seeing very fast the salient features of things: novels, peoples, disciplines and ideas. ... Where Wilson now finds a place in contemporary thought is with the conviction that "man is on the point of an evolutionary leap of consciousness". (King, 2010)

Essays by Colin Wilson on psychology

All bibliographical details extracted from section **C** & **D** of *The Ultimate Colin Wilson Bibliography, 1956–2015* by Colin Stanley (Colin Wilson Studies # 24). Nottingham: Paupers' Press, 2015.

(N) indicates a copy is available to consult in the *Colin Wilson Collection* at the University of Nottingham.

C63. **"The irrational hatred"** in *Cavalier,* vol. 14, no. 138, (December 1964): 69–70. **(N)**

Wilson discussed the way in which we tend to resent the success of those people who we think have not earned it through hard work and gloat over any misfortune that may befall them. He cited our attitude to the death of Ian Fleming and the fall of the British businessman John Bloom as examples.

C64. **"The ends of pain"** in *Town* (December 1964): 47, 110. **(N)**

Wilson attempted to make us "realise ... just how brutal and barbarous life in Europe was only two centuries ago" with descriptions of hideous tortures meted out in front of large crowds of onlookers.

C68. **"Big heart, tiny head"** in *Cavalier,* vol. 15, no. 140, (February 1965): 69–70. **(N)**

Essay, included in "The Big Board", in which Wilson bemoaned the fact that contemporary writers do not think enough. John Osborne comes in for special treatment: "big heart, tiny head"!

C69. **"Selecting a sexual partner"** in *Cavalier,* vol. 15, no. 141, (March 1965): 30–31. **(N)**

Essay in which Wilson asked: Why are most men so unselective about their sexual partners? "Is it surprising that poets complain that love is 50% torment when most marriages are an uncomfortable union of two people who don't really like one another, but are too tied by habit and emotion to break away?"

C70. **"Female body over female mind?"** in *Cavalier,* vol. 15, no. 142, (April 1965): 30–31. **(N)**

Essay included in "The Big Board". Reflecting on the death of Ian Fleming, Wilson asked: does the female body mean more to men than the female mind? "Man-the-Hunter has a new frankness," he wrote, which has culminated in the creation of James Bond, a man who treats women "purely as bed-fodder, as *objects* rather than people". Wilson feels that this attitude is only "one step away from the Marquis de Sade" and that this kind of hero has gone as far as it possibly can without becoming a villain.

C71. **"Symposium"** in *Penthouse,* vol. 1, no.1, (April 1965): 11–14 and 68–69, 71. **(N)**

A panel discussion on the "sexual revolution" with Alan Sillitoe, Laura Del Rivo, Alex Trocchi, Stuart Holroyd, Bill Hopkins, and Wilson. This is the first issue of *Penthouse,* and the only one edited by Bill Hopkins. Wilson was listed as contributing editor.

C72. **"Drugs and creative man"** in *Penthouse,* vol. 1, no. 2, (May 1965): 42–44 and 53. **(N)**

C73. **"The violent void"** in *Cavalier,* vol. 15, no. 144, (June 1965): 64–65. **(N)**

C74. **"The intelligent man's guide to sex"** in *Cavalier,* vol. 15, no. 145, (July 1965): 18–19, 38, 47 and 80–83. **(N)**

C76. **"Sex as catharsis"** in *Cavalier,* vol. 15, no. 147, (September 1965): 66–68. **(N)**

C77. **"Sex in Scandinavia: Once and for all time"** in *Cavalier,* vol. 15, no. 148, (October 1965): 22–23, 58–60 and 69–70. **(N)**

C80A. **"Colin Wilson on sexual snobbery"** in *Punch,* vol. 251, no. 6579, (October 12, 1966): 538–539. **(N)**

As his contribution to the series "The Class Struggle", Wilson considered the peculiarly English attitude to sex "… like Yeats's small boy with his nose pressed to a sweet shop window."

C81. **"Towards a new criminology"** in *Crime and Detection*, no. 2, (November 1966): 11–27. **(N)**

Wilson highlighted the need for a completely new psychology of crime: "… existential psychology which sees crime, neurosis, psychosis and alcoholism as different responses to the same basic problems". He thought that an institute should be set up to study "abnormal" killers (the term "serial killer" not being in use at that time). This anticipates the world's first National Centre for the Analysis of Violent Crime set up in the US during the 1970s. Wilson's desire to understand the psychology of serial killers led to him corresponding with Moors Murderer Ian Brady in the 1990s and encouraging Brady to write *The Gates of Janus*.

C86. **"Existential psychology: A novelist's approach"** in *Challenges of Humanistic Psychology*, edited by James F. T. Bugental. New York: McGraw-Hill, 1967, cloth, pp. 68–78. **(N)**

ab. New York: McGraw-Hill, 1967, paper, pp. 68–78.

b. *The Bicameral Critic*, pp. 38–54.

Phenomenology; The "robot"; The "St. Neot's Margin"; The "orgasm experience"; The "robot" and the "real me"; Consciousness and habit; External stimulation and internal intentionality; "Faculty X"; The spirit/body duality; Beyond the "robot"; Conclusion: man's possible evolution.

C99. **"The dominant five per cent"** in *The Criminologist*, (May-August. 1970): 72–84.

b. in: *Papers from the Criminologist* edited by Nigel Morland. London: Wolfe Pub. Co., cloth, 1971, pp. 231–241.

c. in: *The Criminologist* edited by Nigel Morland. New York: Library Press, 1972, pp. 231–241. **(N)**

C100. **"A universe that thinks?"** in *Illustrated London News* 257, (20 June 1970): 22–23. **(N)**

"It is possible to acknowledge that the range of our senses, and our subconscious knowledge, may be wider than we suppose. If this is an 'information universe' and all living beings are crude attempts at radio sets, then there is no telling what stations your radio might not be picking up by accident."

C108. **"When is a neurotic not a neurotic?"** in *Daily Telegraph Magazine* (2 April 1971): 7. **(N)**

"The correct definition of a neurotic is a man who is weak minded enough to think he needs a psychiatrist."

C110. **"Soundless in solitary"** in *Penthouse*, vol. 6, no.4, (July 1971): 18–20 and 75. **(N)**

b. *The Unexpurgated Penthouse*. London: NEL, 1972, paper, pp. 66–74.

An essay on "black room" experiments: "An utterly silent cell, first devised by the Chinese for brainwashing, may have dramatic potential for medical cures and mental expansion."

C112. **"Freud, Reich, and Nietzsche"** in *The Humanist* 86 (July 1971): 213–214. **(N)**

C113. **"Getting inside the outsiders"** in *T.V. Times* vol. 65, no. 43, (21 October 1971): 12. **(N)**

Fifteen years after *The Outsider*, Wilson felt that more and more intelligent people are reacting against being treated as a cog in a machine.

C117. **"Love as an adventure in mutual freedom"** in *Love Today: A New Exploration*, edited by Herbert A. Otto. New York: Association Press, 1972, cloth, pp. 49–65. **(N)**

b. New York: Dell, 1973, paper, pp. 69–78.

c. in: *The Bicameral Critic*, pp. 55–72.

C119. **"'Dual-value response': A new key to Nietzsche"** in *Malahat Review* 24 (October 1972): 53–66.

b. *The Bicameral Critic*, pp. 95–109. **(N)**

The enigma of Nietzsche; Heidegger on Nietzsche; Nihilism; The "dual-value response"; Examples of this in Nietzsche's life; The "bird's-eye view"; Nietzsche and sex; Parallels with the ideas of Husserl.

C120. **"Dominance and sex"** in *Sexual Behavior 2* (October 1972): n.k.

b. *Sexual Behavior—Current Issues: An Interdisciplinary Perspective*, edited by L. Gross. New York: Spectrum Books, 1974, pp. 127–135. Contains a commentary by Jessie Bernard. **(N)**

C127. **"One of the greatest intellectual advances of the twentieth century: An evaluation of the work of Charlotte Bach"** in *Time Out* no. 164 (13–19 April 1973): 13–15. **(N)**

C128. **"The dominant killer"** in *Men Only*, vol. 38, no. 5, (May 1973), pp. 10–12, 14 and 42. **(N)**

C253. **"Night of the full moon"** in *Men Only,* vol. 39, no. 12, (December 1974): 10–12, 18 and 34. **(N)**

An essay on the effects of the moon.

C263. **"The male menopause"** in *The Male Menopause,* edited by Derek Bowskill and A. Linacre. London: Frederick Müller, 1976, cloth, pp. 117–121.

b. London: Pan Books, 1978, paper, pp. 130–135. **(N)**

C284A. **"Een nieuwe theorie over de ladder der persoonlijkheden in hetzelfde individu"** in *De weg naar een nieuw Bewustzijn: lezingen en discussies tijdens het eerste Bres Symposium gehouden op 22 Oktober 1977 in het Instituut voor de Tropen te Amsterdam.* Den Haag: *Bres,* 1978, pp. 41–58 and 59–69 for the discussion. [Dutch]

Rough translation: "A new theory about the personality ladder within the individual." This is a transcript of a lecture given by Wilson, followed by a discussion, at: "The Path Towards a New Awareness: lectures and discussions during the first *Bres* Symposium held at the Dutch Tropical Institut, Amsterdam, on 22 October, 1977". Those taking part include Professor Dr. G. Quispel, Hubert Lampo, Hélène Ronard, and Wilson.

C291. **"Consciousness and the divided brain"** in *Second Look,* vol. 1, no. 12, (October 1979), pp. 6–11 and 29. **(N)**

Important essay reprinted in *The Essential Colin Wilson* and then as the pamphlet *The Laurel and Hardy Theory of Consciousness.*

C324. **"The real Charlotte"** in *Encounter* vol. 59, no. 3–4 (September/ October 1982): 9–18. **(N)**

An important essay about Charlotte Bach, written after her death in June 1981, when it was discovered that she was a man. Wilson reconsidered her sexual theories in light of this new and startling discovery.

C326. **"Charlotte Bach"** in *Time Out* (13–19 April 1983), pp. 13–15.

C330. **"Peak experience,"** in *Resurgence,* no. 92 (May-June 1982): 8–15 **(N)**

a. as "Peak Experience: The Schumacher Lecture 1982" in *The Schumacher Lectures, Volume 2,* edited by Kumar Satish. **(N)** London: Blond & Briggs, 1984, cloth, pp. 62–96.

b. London: Abacus, 1986, paper, pp. 62–96.

c. in: *The Essential Colin Wilson*, pp. 220–240.

A very important essay for which Wilson wrote a postscript "The Human Condition 1984", in *The Essential Colin Wilson*, pp. 241–248.

C344. **"What the McLuhan message omitted"** in *Hampstead and Highgate Express* (28 June 1985): 81. **(N)**

C348. **"Charlotte's strange evolution"** in *Hampstead and Highgate Express*, (25 October 1985): 81. **(N)**

Another essay about Charlotte Bach.

C350. **"The peaks society must scale"** in *Hampstead and Highgate Express*, (28 December 1985): 9. **(N)**

An article about Maslow in which Wilson looked forward to a time when "… everybody would be born with the ability to induce peak experiences. And the face of our civilisation would be totally changed."

C357. **"Maslow, Sheldrake and the peak experience"** in *Critique: A journal of Conspiracies and Metaphysics*, (Santa Rosa, CA.), issue 21–22, (1986): 72–75. **(N)**

b. in: *Semiotext(e) SF*, edited by Peter Rucker et al. New York: Autonomedia, 1989, paper, pp. 251–254.

c. in: *Ibid*. Edinburgh: AK Press, [n.d.], paper, pp. 251–254. **(N)**

C358. **"The intentional arrow"** in *The Age Monthly Review*, vol. 6, no. 7, (November 1986): 7–9. **(N)**

C363. **"Paranormal phenomena and the unconscious"** in *The Oxford Companion to the Mind*. Oxford: O.U.P., 1987, cloth and paper, pp. 581–583. **(N)**

C384. **"The romantic's dilemma: Insights into the Laurel and Hardy school of consciousness; Part 1"** in *Magical Blend*, (San Francisco), issue 19, (1988): 24–26, 28, 30, 32, 34–36. **(N)**

From a lecture delivered at the California Institute of Integral Studies.

C385. **"The romantic's dilemma: Insights into the Laurel and Hardy school of consciousness; Part 2"** in *Magical Blend*, San Francisco), issue 20, (1988): 28–30, 32–35. **(N)**

Conclusion of above lecture.

C397. **"Sex, crime and the occult"** in *Rapid Eye 1*, edited by Simon Dwyer. Brighton: R.E. Publishing, 1989, paper, pp. 114–118.

b. London: Annihilation Press, 1993, revised and expanded, paper, pp. 424–433. **(N)**

C408. **"Inside the twisted mind of a kidnapper"** in *Evening Standard* (London), (4 February 1992): 9. **(N)**

Article about the kidnapping of Stephanie Slater.

C429. **"Shy sexologist"** in *Abraxas,* no. 9, [1995]: 17–19. **(N)**

An essay about Havelock Ellis.

C430. **"Slouching towards Bethlehem"** in *Abraxas,* no. 9, [1995]: 2–9.

A series of extracts from a forthcoming full-length study of charlatan messiahs. **(N)**

C432. **"The three Christs of Ypsilanti"** in *Abraxas,* no. 10, [1995]: 2–8.

Another extract from the forthcoming study of charlatan messiahs dealing with "one of the most memorable experiments in the history of psychiatry." An experiment which brought together, in the same mental ward, three men who were firmly convinced they were Jesus Christ. **(N)**

C447. **"Like father, like sons"** in *Daily Mail* (30 November 1996): 16.

Fred West and his brother John. **(N)**

C463. **"Hypnosis"** in *Daily Mail* (15 August 1998): 12–13. **(N)**

Wilson asked if it is really possible for one human being to enter the mind of another and then control it—for good or evil. After providing a potted history of the subject he decided that hypnosis "… is an extremely powerful medical tool whose results can be good or bad … [but] … when we come to a fuller understanding of it, I'm sure we will be at the beginning of a new age in medical research."

C499. **"King Rat's death wish"** in *Daily Mail* (20 January 2001): 36–37.

In a fascinating essay, Wilson wrote about his relationship with Ian Brady, labelling him a "self-esteem killer"—highly dominant, embittered by society's refusal to recognise his importance and expressing his resentment in crime. **(N)**

C504. **"Why they can never be free of themselves"** in *Mail on Sunday,* (24 June 2001): n.k.

Article about the release of the killers of James Bulger.

C510. **"The hate that makes a monster"** in *Daily Mail* (14 December 2001): 12. **(N)**

More about the psychology of a paedophile in the wake of Roy Whiting's conviction for the murder of Sarah Payne.

C516. **"A murderous liar and manipulator, but never a victim"** in *Daily Mail* (29 May 2002): 19. **(N)**

Article about the possible release of Myra Hindley.

C517. "Inside the mind of a serial killer" in *Daily Mail* (20 July 2002): 8. **(N)**

Wilson reflected on the case of Dr Harold Shipman

C518. "Are some people born criminal?" in *Daily Mail* (2 August 2002): 12. **(N)**

C519. "Inside the mind of a paedophile" in *Daily Mail* (14 August 2002): 6. **(N)**

As the hunt for the missing schoolgirls Holly Wells and Jessica Chapman continues, Wilson attempted to explain the psychology of people who abduct and sexually assault children.

C520. "Willing convert to a creed of sadism" in *Daily Mail* (16 November 2002): 6–9. **(N)**

Article about Myra Hindley after her death was announced with photographs showing how her physical appearance had changed over the years in jail.

C544. "Piecing together the mind of a murderer" in *Daily Mail* (24 August 2005): 5.

Article about the abduction and murder of schoolboy Rory Blackhall.

C545. "A man beyond redemption" in *Daily Mail* (29 September 2005): 14. **(N)**

Wilson on why Ian Huntley should never be freed.

C549. "Observe the rats: the dominant five per cent have to be tackled" in *The Times* (3 December 2005): 25.

Wilson on the worryingly predictable behaviour of Anthony Walker's killers.

C550. "The big idea" in *Adbusters: Journal of the Mental Environment* #63, vol. 14, no. 1 (Jan/Feb 2006): 3 un-numbered pages. **(N)**

b. as: "The Psychology of Optimism" in *Colin Wilson: Philosopher of Optimism* by Brad Spurgeon, pp. 79–85 **(N)**

c. in *Abraxas Unbound*, vol. 1 (2007): 4–6 **(N)**

C551. "A murder mystery: Why do some killings dominate the headlines?" in *The Times* (28 January 2006): 25.

Wilson on our fixation with the Soham Murders.

C572. "Super consciousness: The quest for the peak experience" in *The Watkins Review*, Issue 22 (Summer 2009): 5. **(N)**

Wilson condensed his new book *Super Consciousness*.

C573. "Hanging him would have been more humane" in *Daily Mail* (23 March 2010): 8. **(N)**

In an article about Ian Huntley, Wilson argued that the death penalty "far from being a form of state-sanctioned viciousness, actually demonstrates greater compassion to both murderer and victims."

"A truly moral society would recognise that no purpose is served by keeping [Huntley] inside."

D6. "Introduction" in *Juvenile Homosexual Experience and Its Effect on Adult Sexuality*, by Robert H. V. Ollendorff. New York: Julian Press, 1966, cloth.

b. London: Tallis Press (Distributed by Luxor Press), 1974, cloth, p. vii-xxi. **(N)**

Wilson's introduction appears only in "b".

D15. "Introduction" in *Geography of Consciousness*, by William Arkle. Sudbury, Suffolk: Neville Spearman, 1974, cloth, pp. 5–22. **(N)**

A review of this book, by Alan Hull Walton, appears in *Books and Bookmen*, vol. 19, no.10 (July 1974) mentioning Wilson at length.

D23. "Introductory note" in *A Report on the Violent Male*, by A. E. van Vogt. St. Austell: Privately printed for Wilson by Francis Anthony Ltd., n.d. [1975], paper, pp. 3–5. **(N)**

b. Nottingham: Paupers' Press, 1992, paper, pp. 1–4. **(N)**

c. Nottingham: Paupers' Press, 1992, cloth, limited edition of 100 numbered copies, pp. 1–4. **(N)**

d. San Bernardino: Borgo Press, 1992, paper, pp. 1–4.

e. Nottingham: Paupers' Press (Uniform Edition), 2008, paper, pp. 3–6 **(N)**

Review: Dexter, Gary. "Surprising literary ventures" in *The Spectator* (1 December 2007): 67.

D58. "Introduction" in *Multiple Man: Explorations in Possession & Multiple Personality* by Adam Crabtree. Toronto: Collins, 1985, cloth, 3 un-numbered pages.

b. London: Holt, Rinehart and Winston, 1985, cloth, un-numbered pages. **(N)**

c. London: Grafton, 1988, paper, pp. 9–12.

D75. "Introduction" in *Educating Psyche: Emotion, Imagination and the Unconscious in Learning* by Bernie Neville. Melbourne, Australia: Collins Dove, 1989, paper, pp. vi–x.

b. Greensborough, Victoria: Flat Chat Press, 2005, paper, pp. 8–11. **(N)**

D90. **"Foreword"** in *Wholeness or Transcendence?* by George Feuerstein. Burdett, NY: Larson Publications/The Paul Brunton Philosophic Foundation, 1992, paper, pp. 9–14. **(N)**

D101. **"Foreword"** in *Quantum Consciousness: The Guide to Experiencing Quantum Psychology* by Stephen Wolinsky. Norfolk, CT: Bramble, 1993, paper, pp. xi–xiv. **(N)**

D110. **"Foreword"** in *Future Visions: The Unpublished Papers of Abraham Maslow* edited by Edward Hoffman. Thousand Oaks, CA: Sage, 1996, cloth, pp. ix–xvi (published simultaneously in trade paperback) **(N)**

D138B. **"Appendix: Personal notes on Maslow"** in *Psychology of Science* by Abraham Maslow. Berkeley, CA: Maurice Bassett, 2002, e-book, pp. 104–121. **(N)**

Wilson's contribution is extracted from his book *New Pathways in Psychology: Maslow and the Post-Freudian Revolution.*

D141. **"Introduction"** in *Out of Time: The Five Laws of Psychological Time and How to Transcend Them* by Steve Taylor. Nottingham: Paupers' Press, 2003, paper, pp. vii–xiv. **(N)**

Review: Newman, Paul. *Abraxas Unbound*, vol. 1 (2007): 111–112.

D143. **"Foreword"** in *A Secret History of Consciousness* by Gary Lachman. Great Barrington, MA: Lindisfarne Books, 2003, trade paper, pp. ix–xix. **(N)**

Notes on Psychology for George Pransky

Colin Wilson

Dear George,[1]

These are the notes I promised you about the psychologists I would regard as your own predecessors.

First of all, the quotation from the philosopher Epictetus. He lived sometime after 50AD, and was a Stoic—at one time a Roman slave, who was given his freedom. He said: "What alarms and disturbs man are not real things, but his opinions and fancies about things."

The tendency towards "mechanical" psychology probably begins with a French philosopher La Mettrie,[2] who in 1748 published a book called *Man the Machine* (*L'homme Machine*). He was trying to demonstrate that man can be explained entirely in mechanical terms, like a penny in the slot machine.

I should add that the hidden motive behind this was a revolt against the Catholic Church, and its dogmas and intellectual tyranny. So I've always had a good deal of sympathy for La Mettrie. He was followed by Condillac[3] and Cabanis.[4] Condillac argued that our so-called mental life is merely a matter of physical sensations, and Cabanis that the brain secretes thoughts as the liver secretes bile.

But for me, the first of the great "positive psychologists"— psychologists who recognised the freedom of the will—was another

Frenchman, Maine de Biran,[5] who flourished around the beginning of the nineteenth century. He was a soldier who retired to a castle in the Dordogne to devote his life to philosophy. Although he started off as a follower of Condillac, he gradually became more and more opposed to this idea that man is nothing more than a penny in the slot machine (The French philosopher Descartes was the original thinker who was responsible for this idea—he saw some elaborate robots driven by water in the gardens of Versailles and was suddenly basically struck with the idea that man is a machine with a soul, whereas animals, he thought, were machines pure and simple).

Anyway, Maine de Biran objected to the idea of man as a pure machine and pointed out that when I'm making some kind of real effort, I have a clear feeling that it is I who am doing it, not a machine. I may feel mechanical when I'm doing something boring or automatic, but as soon as I exert my will, I become aware that I'm not a machine—that I possess an *active* power.

This vital insight could have altered the course of French philosophy, but no one was really interested in pursuing the idea that man possesses free will. It probably struck these philosophers as an attempt to let in religion by the back door.

Immediately after Maine de Biran, the most influential philosopher was Auguste Comte,[6] who created what he called his "positive philosophy" which you and I would regard as totally negative. He thought that the basic trouble with human beings is false belief—superstition—which includes every form of religion, and that once man has turned his back on superstition, we shall have a race of truly free human beings.

Unfortunately, French philosophy—and English philosophy—pursued this more or less mechanistic line of Condillac and Comte, and it was developed in England by John Stewart Mill, and later by Herbert Spencer. And of course, then Freud came along, and although he deeply shocked the late Victorians, his philosophy was really, in fact, as mechanistic as Condillac's. Man is nothing more than a helpless puppet in the hands of his unconscious mind, over which he has no power whatever. Freud recognised that this philosophy was deeply pessimistic, but said that, unfortunately, that was the truth about the universe and we had to accept it.

In fact the next great "positive psychologist" after Maine de Biran was William James,[7] who began to believe in the importance of free will as a result of an appalling experience which almost cost him his sanity. As a young man who had received a brilliant education, James suddenly found himself in the position of not knowing where he wanted to go or what he wanted to do. As you know, this feeling of total uncertainty about yourself and your future leads to a kind of inner collapse. Man actually recharges his vital batteries by the activity of his will, and if this activity ceases as a result of pessimism or total lack of purpose, he begins to run down. He falls into the hands of the mechanical part of the mind (and body)—which I have called "the robot".

We all possess this mechanical servant whose business is to do things for us. So you learn to do something—like riding a bicycle or skiing or driving a car or talking French—painfully and slowly, and then suddenly the robot takes over, and does it far more efficiently than you could do it.

The problem is that the robot not only does the things you want him to do—like driving a car—but also the things you don't want him to do. You go for a walk which you find marvellous and magical, but the third or fourth time you go for the same walk, it is already the robot taking the walk instead of you. You hear a piece of music that moves you deeply, but by the time you hear it for the third or fourth time, it is the robot listening instead of you (I've even said that I have caught him making love to my wife).

And when we get rather fed up or discouraged, we cease to put so much effort into life, with the result that the robot tends to take over.

Now there is one basic problem about the robot. He does not recharge your vital batteries in the same way that you do yourself. When what you might call "the real you" is doing something, giving it your full and enthusiastic attention, you put a tremendous charge into your batteries. But when the robot does things, it hardly charges the batteries at all. This is why people fall into that state of boredom and misery that William James describes.

James goes on to describe how, in this state of low vitality and self-doubt, he went into a room at twilight when there suddenly appeared to his mind's eye the image of an idiot he had seen recently in a mental home. This man had a greenish face and long black hair and was staring blankly in front of him. James suddenly had the horrifying thought: "If the hour should strike for me as it struck for him, nothing I could do could possibly save me from this fate." He said that it was this sudden perception of the merely momentary discrepancy between himself and the idiot that filled him with horror, and caused a kind of inner collapse. From then on, he could do nothing of any importance.

He also became totally convinced that Condillac was right, and that man is merely a machine. Everything we do is directed by some motive, and can therefore be regarded as mechanical.

This thought depressed him profoundly until one day he read the work of a French philosopher called Charles Renouvier,[8] who remarked that, although most of the things we do can be explained in purely mechanical terms, there is one thing which obviously demonstrated our free will: we can *think* one thought rather than another. And as James thought about this, it suddenly struck him that this is obviously true. You can change the direction of your thoughts as often as you like. This totally convinced James of the reality of free will, and from that moment onwards, he began to recover his mental balance and sense of health.

In my own opinion, James's most important work is an essay called "The Energies of Men", in which he begins by commenting that we're all familiar with the sensation of feeling more or less alive on different days. On some days, he says, we feel as if a cloud weighed upon us,

> "... keeping us below our highest notch of clearness in discernment, sureness in reasoning, or firmness in deciding. Compared to what we ought to be, we are only half awake. Our fires are damped, our drafts are checked. We are making use of only a small part of our possible mental and physical resources.
>
> In some persons this sense of being cut off from their rightful resources is extreme, and we then get the formidable neurasthenic and psychasthenic conditions, with life grown into one tissue of impossibilities, that so many medical books describe.
>
> Stating the thing broadly, the human individual thus lives usually far below his limits; he possesses powers of various sorts which he habitually fails to use. He energises below his maximum and he behaves below his optimum. In elementary faculty, in coordination, in power of inhibition and control, in every conceivable way, his life is contracted like the field of vision of an hysteric subject—but with less excuse, for the poor hysteric is diseased, while in the rest of us it is only an inveterate *habit*—the habit of inferiority to our full self—that is bad.

As you can see at a glance, this is very close to your own ideas. It is our thoughts, our ideas about ourselves that keep us trapped in the lower level of vitality.

I won't go on quoting James's essay—you really ought to read it for yourself. It is tremendously important.

After James, the next most important "positive psychologist" is, in my opinion, the Frenchman Pierre Janet.[9] He was a contemporary of Freud who, in my own view, is a far greater psychologist than Freud.

Janet argued that the most important characteristic of human beings is what he called "the reality function". When we are feeling happy and full of vitality, everything seems much more real. When the reality function becomes weaker, things become less real—they become dreamlike.

Janet made an important distinction between what he calls "psychological force" and "psychological tension".

Psychological force is merely brute strength—the kind of strength that a ditch digger needs to wheel a barrowload of concrete. It is when you *focus* your psychological force on some aim or objective that it turns into something far more creative—psychological *tension.* Sick people are people who have lost their psychological tension.

Psychological tension is obviously the vital energy that William James was talking about. It is what a racing driver experiences as he drives at 100mph. It is a total certainty of his own freedom.

By far the best discussion of Janet is a long chapter in Henri Ellenberger's book *The Discovery of the Unconscious* [1970].

As you know, Abraham Maslow also came to make the same discovery. And when he wrote to me in about 1958, I was tremendously struck by his basic observation that all healthy people have, with great frequency, what Maslow called "peak experiences"—sudden overwhelming happiness or joy. They are, in short, moments in which we exercise the reality function.

Maslow collected many of these from students—one, for example, told him how, when he was working his way through college as a jazz drummer, he suddenly found himself one night drumming so perfectly that he couldn't do a thing wrong. At that moment he went into the peak experience.

William James had made much the same comment. He said that a ball player can suddenly, in certain moods, find himself playing so perfectly that *the game is playing him.*

These are moments in which our vital energies work with super efficiency.

But Maslow's most important observation, to my mind, is his comment that, when his students began to talk to one another about their peak experiences, *they began to have peak experiences all the time*. As soon as their thoughts became positive, they began to induce it themselves.

In other words, peak experiences are actually *prevented* by the mechanistic view in which we fail to recognise our own potential powers. Talking about peak experiences, Maslow's students made an important discovery. You always have far more vital power than you recognise. We are always allowing our consciousness to fall into the hands of the robot. Any kind of vital effort, or any kind of enthusiasm, pushes us above this robotic threshold and we suddenly become aware of our basic freedom.

The French novelist Proust made the same experience the basis of his enormous novel *Á la Recherche du Temps Perdu*.[10] His hero describes how, when he was feeling tired and dispirited one day, his mother offered him a little cake called a *madeleine*, dipped in herb tea. This suddenly brought back memories of his childhood, with such intensity that he was completely overwhelmed. He wrote: "I had ceased to feel mediocre, accidental, mortal." In other words, Proust realised that he had an immense source of peak experiences inside himself, and the enormous novel is an attempt to recover some of them. In that sense, in spite of Proust's natural pessimism, it is one of the most optimistic novels ever written.

Oddly enough, Maslow never attacked Freud—in spite of the fact that his own ideas were about as far from Freud as it is possible to get.

After Maslow, my next major insight into "positive psychology" came from an American doctor called Howard Miller.[11] Miller declared that we have a kind of centre in the brain which he called "the unit of pure thought". You might call it the freedom centre.

Miller said: "Imagine that you are on a beach on a marvellous hot day, running your feet through the sand and listening to the sound of waves. Now change the image, and imagine that you are standing on a slope covered in snow on a freezing winter day, with all the branches of the trees around you loaded with snow."

Howard then went on to ask: What is it in *us* that enables us to simply switch from a beach on a hot day to a hillside on a freezing day? He says that we fail to recognise this element of freedom inside us. We take it for granted that it is something automatic, and it is nothing of the sort.

He has a very good image to illustrate what he means. He says: Imagine that you are sitting in a cinema, and there is obviously something wrong with the film—it is running badly, and sometimes even upside-down. Finally, you decide to go up to the projection box to see what the hell the projectionist is doing. And when you get there you discover it is empty. And then suddenly you remember: *you* are the projectionist.

In other words, we get too used to allowing the robot to take over our everyday activities, and forget that *we* are the projectionist.

I was always struck by a passage in a short story by Hemingway called "Soldier's Home".[12] It describes a soldier coming back home to his small town in the Mid-West after the First World War, and how bored he gets as he hangs around the pool hall, and exchanges stories with the other people who are standing around, as bored as himself. And Hemingway then says something like: "He remembered all those times during the war, times of crisis when you had done the one thing, the only thing, and it had always come out right." These are, of course, the moments of "the reality function".

The comparison I used was this. Imagine that, for some reason, you have got used to driving your car sitting in the passenger seat, and reaching over to turn the steering wheel. You get so used to this inefficient way of driving that you forget there is any other way—until some emergency occurs, whereupon you quite automatically spring into the driver's seat, and find that you are driving perfectly.

All these images illustrate the same point. We have lost our sense of freedom, because we have allowed ourselves to fall into the hands of the robot. Any kind of emergency will snap us out of this state, and make us aware of our freedom. I also meant to mention the work of Dan MacDougald.[13] I told you about this briefly over the phone, and you will also find a bit about it in my *New Pathways in Psychology*.[14] Dan was a lawyer who lived in Georgia and one day a group of local farmers asked him to fight a case for them. The state authority wanted to flood some land as a reservoir, but it was extremely good farming land. The farmers objected; there was another valley nearby that contained extremely bad land which would be far more suitable. Dan thought that it would be perfectly easy to persuade the authorities, since the case was so reasonable. To his absolute bafflement, he found that he could simply not get through to them. It was like shouting at deaf ears. And it cost years of effort and a vast amount of money to finally achieve what he felt should have been achieved in the first week.

Then he read that experiment with the cat's aural nerve, which I described to you. (I forgot who did this—I think I told you it was a man called Jerome Bruner, but I think I've got it wrong.) Bruner connected the cat's aural nerve—between the eardrum and the brain—up to an oscilloscope, so that when you rang a bell in the cat's ear, the oscilloscope needle would move across the dial. But he discovered that when a cage with a mouse was put in front of the cat, it concentrated so hard on the mouse that you could ring the bell in its ear and the oscilloscope would not budge. The cat was somehow cutting out the sound of the bell *at the eardrum*.

MacDougald came to the conclusion that habitual criminals do the same kind of thing. Rather like Scrooge in Dickens's *A Christmas Carol*, they go around in a state of hatred and resentment, which causes them to "cut out" half of the nice things about being alive "at the eardrum". And yet he discovered that a large percentage of his prisoners were intelligent enough to understand this when it was explained to them, so that they were able to reverse this effect and cease to be habitual criminals.

One of them was the son of George Wallace, one time Governor of Georgia, and he had got into a quarrel with a fellow prisoner in which he felt the only thing he could do in order to "maintain face" was to kill him. Then he attended one of MacDougald's lectures, and immediately realised that this was a stupid thing to do—that he would spend the rest of his life in jail for no particular purpose. And so he simply walked up to his "enemy" in the canteen and said: "Can I buy you a cup of coffee?" The man looked at him with astonishment and then said: "Sure." And instantly, the whole problem simply dissolved away.

MacDougald told me that he had succeeded in rehabilitating about eighty per cent of what he called "hard-core psychopaths" with this kind of treatment. And, incredibly, the Georgia state authorities suddenly decided to stop his treatment! Another example of this habitual deafness!

Of course, what MacDougald was doing in effect, was exactly what the ghosts of Christmas past, etc., were doing to Scrooge—removing the blockages from his ears, and causing him to "open up".

This is only a brief and incomplete account of what I would regard as "positive psychology" of the kind Syd Banks[15] stumbled on. You'll also find a great deal more of this in my *New Pathways in Psychology*.

Notes

1. Dr. George S. Pransky (dates not known) New York psychiatrist and author of *The Renaissance of Psychology* (1998). See the postscript of Colin Wilson's *Super Consciousness* (2009) for his account of how he "discovered" Pransky's work and, through him, that of Sydney Banks. www.pranskyandassociates.com/
2. Julien Offray de La Mettrie (1709–1751).
3. Étienne Bonnot de Condillac (1757–1808).
4. Pierre Jean George Cabanis (1757–1808).
5. Marie François Pierre Maine de Biran (1766–1824).
6. Auguste [Marie François Xavier] Comte (1798–1857).
7. William James (1842–1910).
8. Charles Bernard Renouvier (1815–1903).
9. Pierre Janet (1859–1947).
10. Marcel Proust (1871–1922). *Á la Recherche du Temps Perdu* was published in seven parts between 1913 and 1927.
11. Dates not known but he is presumably Howard B. Miller, author of the paper "What is thought?" published in the journal *Fields Within Fields*, Vol. 13, 1974, 34–37, which describes "... pure thought as an inner observer-thinker unit of ourselves ..." and considers an "... individual's ability and responsibility to take control over his or her evolution ..."
12. Refers to Ernest Hemingway's short story first published in a collection entitled *In Our Time* in 1925.
13. Dates not known. There is an interesting interview, with Judge Asa Kelley, talking about MacDougald's methods of prisoner rehabilitation at: www.youtube.com/watch?v=Rv_nQAYIN1w
14. London: Victor Gollancz, 1972.
15. Sydney Banks (1931–2009) www.sydneybanks.org/See again Colin Wilson's postscript to *Super Consciousness*.

Remembering the outsider: Colin Wilson 1931–2013

Colin Stanley

The philosopher and author Colin Wilson has died at the age of eighty-two. Shortly after his eightieth birthday, in the summer of 2011, when he was due to attend the opening of his archive at the University of Nottingham in the UK, he suffered a stroke from which he never fully recovered. In late October 2013, he was admitted to hospital, near his home in Cornwall in the West of England, suffering from pneumonia and died peacefully at 10.45pm (GMT) on Thursday 5 December with his wife Joy and daughter Sally at his bedside.

He had always intended to live at least as long as his great hero George Bernard Shaw but, sadly, fell well short. However, in a working life as a professional author, spanning over fifty-five years, he produced an awe-inspiring body of work: 181 books; 600 essays and articles for a variety of magazines and newspapers; 162 introductions to other authors' works; and over 350 book reviews. As his bibliographer I have struggled to keep pace with his output over the years; a fact that never ceased to amuse him: he once said that I would be glad when he eventually died so that I could then, at last, produce the definitive edition. But I shall never be in a position to achieve this because I am constantly discovering items of which I was previously unaware and appreciations of his contributions to consciousness studies and philosophy continue to appear in print.

Colin Wilson was born on 26 June 1931 in the East Midlands city of Leicester—the first child of Arthur and Annetta Wilson. At the age of eleven he attended Gateway Secondary Technical School, where his interest in science began to blossom. Even at this early age he seemed to be blessed with the self-confidence and optimistic belief in his own genius that later was often mistaken for arrogance:

> Secretly I admired Newton, for I imagined him as occupying a place in the hierarchy—Archimedes, Galileo, Newton, Planck, Einstein—which would one day include myself.

By the age of fourteen he had compiled a multi-volume work of essays covering all aspects of science entitled "A Manual of General Science". But by the time he left school at sixteen, his interests were already switching to literature. His discovery of George Bernard Shaw's work, particularly *Man and Superman*, was an important landmark. He started to write stories, plays, and essays in earnest—a long "sequel" to *Man and Superman* made him consider himself to be "Shaw's natural successor". After two unfulfilling jobs—one as a laboratory assistant at his old school—he drifted into the Civil Service, but found little to occupy his time.

In the autumn of 1949, he was drafted into the Royal Air Force but soon found himself clashing with authority, eventually feigning homosexuality in order to be dismissed. Upon leaving he took up a succession of menial jobs, spent some time wandering around Europe, and finally returned to Leicester in 1951. There he married his first wife, (Dorothy) Betty Troop, and moved to London, where a son was born. But the marriage rapidly disintegrated as he drifted in and out of several unrewarding jobs. During this traumatic period Colin Wilson was continually working and reworking the novel that was eventually published as *Ritual in the Dark* (1960). He also met three young writers who became close friends—Bill Hopkins, Stuart Holroyd, and Laura Del Rivo. Another trip to Europe followed, and he spent some time in Paris attempting to sell magazine subscriptions.

Returning to Leicester again, he met Joy Stewart—later to become his second wife and mother of their three children—who accompanied him to London. There he continued to work on *Ritual in the Dark*, receiving some advice from Angus Wilson (no relation)—then Deputy Superintendent of the British Museum's Reading Room—and famously slept rough (in a sleeping bag) on Hampstead Heath to save money.

On Christmas Day, 1954, alone in his room, he sat down on his bed and began to write in his journal. He described his feelings as follows:

> It struck me that I was in the position of so many of my favour-ite characters in fiction: Dostoevsky's Raskolnikov, Rilke's Malte Laurids Brigge, the young writer in Hamsun's *Hunger*: alone in my room, feeling totally cut off from the rest of society. It was not a position I relished ... Yet an inner compulsion had forced me into this position of isolation. I began writing about it in my journal, trying to pin it down. And then, quite suddenly, I saw that I had the makings of a book. I turned to the back of my journal and wrote at the head of the page: "Notes for a book *The Outsider in Literature* ...

And so his first, and most famous, book *The Outsider* was conceived—a book that has, to date, been translated into over thirty languages and never been out of print in England, the US, and Japan. He continued to work on it at a furious pace and:

> One day I typed out the introduction, and a few pages from the middle, and sent them to Victor Gollancz with a letter giving a syn-opsis of the book. He replied within 2 days, saying he would be interested to see the book when completed ...

It was eventually published on Monday, 28 May 1956, to tremendous critical acclaim and Colin Wilson's career was well and truly underway. When the fickle critics decided to attack his next book, *Religion and the Rebel* (essentially *The Outsider*, Part 2) in 1957, he had already moved with Joy to Cornwall. Away from the inevitable distractions of London, he settled down to his life's work: "The critics tried to take back what they'd written [but] they couldn't take back the passport they'd given me," he wrote some time later.

He always remained unshakably convinced of his own talent but admitted that, due to economic circumstances, he *was* forced to write too much. Those critics who have failed to see and appreciate that talent are invariably those who have been intimidated by such a vast body of work and unable to distinguish between his ephemeral and essential books. This has become apparent when reading many of the obituaries published since his death, which concentrate on *The Outsider*, its sequel *Religion and the Rebel*, and nothing much beyond. But the truth is that *The Outsider* was just the first volume in what became known as "The Outsider Cycle"—a series of six books that concluded with *Beyond the Outsider* (1965) and was summarised by *Introduction to the New Existentialism* (1966). When the latter was reprinted in 1980 as *The New Existentialism*, he wrote in a newly penned introduction: "If I have contributed anything to existentialism—or, for that matter, to twentieth-century thought in general, here it is. I am willing to stand or fall by it." During this very productive period in the 1960s, Colin Wilson would often accompany a non-fiction book with a novel—his way of putting his philosophical ideas into action. Many of these important and entertaining novels of ideas, written in a variety of genres—*Ritual In the Dark* (1960), *Man Without a Shadow* (1963), *The World of Violence* (1963), *Necessary Doubt* (1964), *The Glass Cage* (1966), *The Philosopher's Stone* (1969), *God of the Labyrinth* (1970)—have recently been rediscovered and returned to print by Valancourt Books. England, however, does not have a tradition of philosopher-novelists and, as a result, his fiction has never been given the credit it is undoubtedly due in this country. When *Ritual In the Dark* was published in French (1962) by Gallimard, for example, the book was hailed as one of the most important novels by a young writer since the war; one critic even declared him as "the natural successor of Lawrence, Huxley and Orwell".

Colin Wilson's optimistic "new existentialism" was a bold move at a time when pessimism held sway in Western philosophy and it is to his credit that he was prepared to stick his neck out and swim against the flow. Despite the French existentialists, he was convinced that we live in a *meaningful* universe and that mankind is heading toward a new phase in its evolution. His "Outsiders"—obsessed as they were with those *moments of vision* in which they achieve a glimpse of this meaning but then become depressed in the cold light of day when they cannot repeat the experience—were pointers towards this higher state of consciousness, which he saw as our birthright. A catalyst, however, was necessary to move beyond the Outsider and bring this about.

In *The Age of Defeat* (1959)—book three of "The Outsider Cycle"—he bemoaned the loss of the hero in twentieth-century life and literature; convinced that we were becoming embroiled in what he termed "the fallacy of insignificance". It was this theory that encouraged the celebrated American psychologist Abraham Maslow to contact him in

1963. The two corresponded regularly and met on several occasions before Maslow's death in 1970. A biography and assessment of his work, *New Pathways in Psychology: Maslow and the Post-Freudian Revolution*, based on audiotapes that Maslow had provided, was written by Colin Wilson and published in 1972. Maslow's observation of "peak experiences" in his students—those sudden moments of overwhelming happiness that we all experience from time to time—provided Colin Wilson with an important clue in his search for the mechanism that might control these "moments of vision". Maslow, however, was convinced that "peak experiences" could not be induced; Colin Wilson thought otherwise.

At a time when experimentation with mind-altering drugs was prevalent, Colin Wilson, once again, had the strength to contradict. His own unfortunate mescalin experience (detailed in an appendix to *Beyond the Outsider*) confirmed to him that short cuts to heightened consciousness were not in any way satisfactory. Rather, he advocated a mental discipline based on his interpretation of Edmund Husserl's theory of intentionality, asserting that to live much more vital and appreciative lives we need to learn how to fire our attention at the world out there in order to see it not through a glass, darkly, as we invariably do at present, but as it *actually is*. When all is said and done, it is in this field of consciousness studies, that his true legacy lies.

In the late 1960s Colin Wilson was offered his first commission: a book about the occult. Up until then he had always anticipated trends in thought and literature rather than being one for jumping on to bandwagons. In 1961, for example, he published, with Pat Pitman, *The Encyclopaedia of Murder*, a book which anticipated the boom in true crime studies by almost twenty years. His *The Strength to Dream*—the fourth in "The Outsider Cycle", a book on literature and imagination published in 1962—heralded the late 1960s' obsession with fantasy and science fiction literature. The late 1960s also brought about a surge in interest in all things mystical, and on this occasion Wilson was not altogether ahead of the game: the pioneers were Louis Pauwels and Jacques Bergier whose *The Morning of the Magicians* had been a bestseller in France for several years. His publishers clearly wanted Wilson to replicate its success in the English-speaking world and he did not disappoint them: his study *The Occult* (1971) went on to be a bestseller and an inspiration to many who read it. Although it lost him some readers who felt that he had abandoned the rigours of philosophy for a far less "worthy" subject, he gained many, many more.

In fact, Colin Wilson had not abandoned philosophy at all. Indeed, he always considered his "serious" occult books to be a logical extension of his "new existentialism", providing evidence that man possesses latent powers which, if tapped and harnessed, could lead to hugely expanded consciousness and potentially even an evolutionary leap. He went on to write two more large books on the subject: *Mysteries: An Investigation into the Occult, the Paranormal and the Supernatural* (1978) and *Beyond the Occult* (1988) which came to be known as his "Occult Trilogy" and are now acknowledged classics in the field of the occult sciences. The three books amounted to a monumental 1600 pages and spawned many other lesser works on the subject.

His longstanding interest in criminology, in particular the "motive-less murder" carried out by serial killers, culminated in the hugely impressive *A Criminal History of Mankind* (1984). He was always prob-ing to understand the psychology of those "negative" Outsiders who chose to channel their frustrations with society in this way. After deliv-ering a lecture in a Philadelphia jail in 1973, he was convinced that prisoners should be rewarded not just for good conduct but for being creative and making good use of their period of incarceration. To this end he corresponded for many years with Moors Murderer Ian Brady, finally persuading him to write a book instead of focusing his frustra-tions on the prison authorities. He found a publisher for it—*The Gates of Janus* (2001)—and even wrote an introduction, much to the scorn of the tabloid press.

In 2003, Colin Wilson completed his four-volume science fantasy epic *Spider World* and, latterly, became interested in prehistory, specu-lating that civilisation was many thousands of years older than is cur-rently believed. He wrote three books on this subject: *From Atlantis to the Sphinx* (1996), *The Atlantis Blueprint* (with Rand Flem-Ath, 2000), and *Atlantis and the Kingdom of the Neanderthals* (2006).

He was an extraordinary man with an exceptionally intelligent mind, capable of thinking "out of the box". Iris Murdoch famously tried to convince him of the benefits of a university education but wisely he resisted, preferring to draw his own conclusions from his extensive (and intensive) reading and research. There were always plans for several possible books in his head and he would invariably enjoy outlining them to guests at his home either over a glass of good wine (about which he also wrote: *A Book of Booze*, in 1974) or on the walk he took for exercise every afternoon after a hard days' work. His generosity was legendary: the fact that he made time to write so many introductions to other authors' works, usually with no thought of any reward, speaks for itself. He was also an excellent and popular speaker who had the ability to talk on his subject for well over an hour using no notes.

In the summer of 2013 I went to his home in Cornwall, with a representative from the University of Nottingham's Department of Manuscripts, to collect seventy-five of his manuscripts and take them into safe-keeping at the university's archive store. Another such trip was made in the summer of 2015 to collect more manuscripts, journals, and correspondence. These now sit alongside a huge collection of his printed work and it is hoped that this will become a hub for Wilson Studies in the future. On 1 July 2016 the "First international Colin Wilson conference" was held there with delegates and speakers from all over the globe.

Colin Wilson is survived by his second wife (Pamela) Joy, their three children: Sally, Damon, and Rowan; Roderick, a son from his previous marriage, and a total of nine grandchildren. Following a service of celebration for his life, attended by family members and friends, his body was interred in the churchyard of St Goran in Cornwall, near to his home, on Friday 20 December 2013.

There was a Memorial Service held, in celebration of his life and work, at St. James' Church, Piccadilly, London, on 14 October 2014. Speakers included Gary Lachman, Laura Del Rivo, Guy Lyon Playfair, Donald Rumbelow, Nicolas Tredell, Damon Wilson, and myself. Music was provided by Kerenza Peacock, Howard Blake, and Mike Servent.

* * *

Entry from Colin Wilson's journal
(read by Colin Stanley at his memorial service)

Saturday 7 October 1995

Earlier this week I had a brilliant and central insight. Yet this morning, trying to recall it, I was totally unable—or rather, I could only get it in flashes. Luckily, I knew I had it on tape. And I rewound the tape and hit the precise spot in one go.

It was this. Why is it that moods of happiness and intensity make us sigh with *relief*, as if we've seen something that takes a load off our minds?

What happens is that we suddenly see the reality of things. We are usually trapped in a narrow room inside our own heads—Svidrigailov's room (from *Crime and Punishment*). We see things merely as symbols—that's a doorknob, that's a tree ... But we don't *feel* they are real. Then we set out on holiday, and the glass bubble that encloses us goes "pop", like a sinus clearing ("Suddenly I can breathe again"), and we really see things as individuals, and feel almost as if they are communicating with us.

I used this on my walk in Scotland Woods on Wednesday. I looked at things, and thought: "You are real, and I want to see you in your reality." And I kept on getting flashes of seeing things as real—getting outside my own head.

This is why going to the cinema sometimes "freed" me in my teens—I got "absorbed", and the glass bubble popped and released me.

This is also what happened at Teignmouth, and in Cheltenham when I found Sally—that feeling of relief that meant that now I could afford to give my attention to anything I wanted, like reading a book slowly and carefully, or enjoying a leisurely meal.

This "relief" could also be compared to a frightened child who thinks he has lost his mother—then he sees her, and rushes into her arms. The "holiday feeling" actually gives us a sense of "belonging", of being surrounded by benevolence.

Another point: the sense of being "on top" of things. The same morning as writing the above (yesterday), I went into the kitchen at 6.30 to make tea (I now make a habit of getting up early—in the summer I was occasionally up at 5—and getting some reading done before I go in to Joy at 8), and thought: "Oh, good, I got some Darjeeling tea bags from Tesco yesterday"—the previous day I'd had to make my tea with a much stronger variety. And this thought was enough to give me a sense of a "lifting of the heart" and being "on top of things". On a bigger scale, finding Sally in Cheltenham did the same. We tend to go around in a basically robotic state, which is of "indifference", so we are inclined to fear "problems". (In my teens I seemed to have a kind of inner sinking feeling most of the time, the feeling that something was bound to go wrong.) This feeling of being "on top" has the quality of an *insight*, a recognition that there is something wrong with normal consciousness—that is: this neutral state that so easily slips into anxiety and fear ... There is sufficient insight here, I think, to provide meditation for a whole day.

FURTHER READING

Braine, J. *Room at the Top*. London: Eyre & Spottiswoode, 1957.

Cartland, B. *Sex and the Teenager*. London: Frederick Muller, 1964.

Cozzens, J G. *By Love Possessed*. New York: Harcourt, Brace, 1957.

Hopkins, B. *The Divine and the Decay*. London: MacGibbon & Kee, 1957.

Hudson, T. J. *The Law of Psychic Phenomena*. New York: G. P. Putnam's, 1893.

Jones, J. *From Here to Eternity*. New York: Charles Scribner's Sons, 1951.

Ollendorff, R. *Juvenile Homosexual Experience and its Effect on Adult Sexuality*. London: Tallis Press, 1974.

Reich, I. O. *Wilhelm Reich: A Personal Biography*. London: Elek, 1969.

Riesman, D. *The Lonely Crowd*. New Haven: Yale UP, 1950.

Stanley, C. *Colin Wilson's "Occult Trilogy": a guide for students*. Winchester: Axis Mundi, 2013.

Van Vogt, A. E. *A Report on the Violent Male*. Nottingham: Paupers' Press, 1992.

Whyte, W. H. *The Organization Man*. New York: Simon and Schuster, 1956.

Wilson, C. *Beyond the Outsider*. London: Arthur Barker, 1965.

Wilson, C. *The Black Room*. London: Weidenfeld & Nicolson, 1971.

Wilson, C. *"Comments on Boredom" and "Evolutionary Humanism and the New Psychology": two unpublished essays*. Nottingham: Paupers' Press, 2013. (Edited and with an introduction by Vaughan Rapatahana).

Wilson, C. *The Craft of the Novel*. London: Victor Gollancz, 1975.

Wilson, C. *The Devil's Party: A History of Charlatan Messiahs*. London: Virgin, 2000.

Wilson, C. *The Essential Colin Wilson*. London: Harrap, 1985.

Wilson, C. *Hesse—Reich—Borges*. Philadelphia: Leaves of Grass Press, 1974.

Wilson, C. *Introduction to "The Faces of Evil": An Unpublished Book*. Nottingham: Paupers' Press, 2013. (Edited and with an introduction by Vaughan Rapatahana).

Wilson, C. *Introduction to the New Existentialism*. London: Hutchinson, 1966.

Wilson, C. *The Laurel and Hardy Theory of Consciousness*. Mill Valley, CA: Robert Briggs, 1986.

Wilson, C. *Mysteries: An Investigation into the Occult, the Paranormal and the Supernatural*. London: Hodder & Stoughton, 1978.

Wilson, C. *Notes on Psychology for George Pransky*. St Austell: Abraxas, 2001. (See Appendix 1).

Wilson, C. *Order of Assassins: The Psychology of Murder*. London: Rupert Hart-Davis, 1972.

Wilson, C. *The Personality Surgeon*. Sevenoaks, Kent: New English Library, 1985.

Wilson, C. *The Philosopher's Stone*. London: Arthur Barker, 1969.

Wilson, C. *Wilhelm Reich*. London: Village Press, 1974.

Wouk, H. *The Caine Mutiny*. New York: Doubleday, 1951.

Colin Wilson Studies

A series of books on the life and work of Colin Wilson written by experts and scholars worldwide. Published by Paupers' Press.
ISSN: 0959–180-X. Series Editor: Colin Stanley

1. Moorhouse, J., & Newman, P. *Colin Wilson, Two Essays: "The English Existentialist" and "Spiders and Outsiders" (including an interview with the author)*.
2. Stanley, C. *"The Nature of Freedom" and Other Essays*.
3. Trowell, M. *Colin Wilson, the Positive Approach: A Response to a Critic*.
4. Smalldon, J. *Human Nature Stained: Colin Wilson and the Existential Study of Modern Murder*.
5. Dalgleish, T. *The Guerilla Philosopher: Colin Wilson and Existentialism*.
6. Lachman, G. *Two Essays on Colin Wilson: "World Rejection and Criminal Romantics" & "From Outsider to Post-Tragic Man"*.
7. Newman, P. *Murder as an Antidote for Boredom: The Novels of Laura Del Rivo, Colin Wilson and Bill Hopkins*.

8. Shand, J., & Lachman, G. *"Colin Wilson as Philosopher" and "Faculty X, Consciousness and the Transcendence of Time"*.

9. Dossor, H. *The Philosophy of Colin Wilson: Three Perspectives*.

10. Stanley, C. *The Work of Colin Wilson: An Annotated Bibliography & Guide. Supplement to 1995*.

11. Robertson, V. *Wilson as Mystic*.

12. Greenwell, T. *Chepstow Road: A Literary Comedy in Two Acts*.

13. Stanley, C. *Colin Wilson, the First Fifty Years: An Existential Bibliography, 1956–2005*. Limited edition of 100 numbered copies. Now out of print.

14. Wilson, C. *"The Death of God" and Other Plays*. Limited edition of 100 numbered copies. Now out of print.

15. Stanley, C. *Colin Wilson's "Outsider Cycle": A Guide for Students*.

16. Wilson, C. *Existential Criticism: Selected Book Reviews* (Edited by Colin Stanley). Limited edition of 100 numbered copies.

17. Stanley, C. *The Colin Wilson Bibliography, 1956–2010*. Limited edition of 50 copies. Now out of print.

18. Diller, A. *Stuart Holroyd: Years of Anger and Beyond*.

19. Campion, S. R. *The Sound Barrier: A Study of the Ideas of Colin Wilson*. Limited edition of 100 numbered copies.

20/1. Daly, A. *The Outsider-Writer, volume 1: Wilson, Camus, Powys, Pessoa, Gadda*.

20/2. Daly, A. *The Outsider-Writer, volume 2: Walser, Jabès, Cendrars, Britton, Home, Céline*.

21. Wilson, C. *Comments on Boredom* and *Evolutionary Humanism and the New Psychology*.

22. Wilson, C. *Introduction to "The Faces of Evil": An Unpublished Book*.

23. Stanley, C. *Colin Wilson's Existential Literary Criticism: A Guide for Students*.

24. Stanley, C. *The Ultimate Colin Wilson Bibliography, 1956–2015*.

25. Tredell, N. *Novels to Some Purpose: The Fiction of Colin Wilson*.

Works by Colin Stanley

Novels

First Novel (2000).
Novel 2 (2005).

Poetry

Sense-less: Complete Nonsense Poetry (2003) with illustrations by Maggie Guillon and Yvonne Harrison.

Non-fiction

The *"Aylesford Review", 1955–1968: An Index* (1984).
Colin Wilson, a Celebration: Essays and Recollections (1988).
The Work of Colin Wilson: An Annotated Bibliography and Guide (1989).
"The Nature of Freedom" and Other Essays (1990).
The Work of Colin Wilson: An Annotated Bibliography and Guide—Supplement to 1995 (2000).
Colin Wilson, the First Fifty Years: An Existential Bibliography 1956–2005 (2006).
Colin Wilson's "Outsider Cycle": A Guide for Students (2009).
Around the Outsider: Essays Presented to Colin Wilson on the Occasion of his 80th Birthday (2011).
The Colin Wilson Bibliography, 1956–2010 (2011).
Colin Wilson's Occult Trilogy: A Guide for Students (2013).
Colin Wilson's Existential Literary Criticism: A Guide for Students (2014).
The Ultimate Colin Wilson Bibliography, 1956–2015 (2015).

REFERENCES

Baker, R. (1988). Sexual outsiders. *Gay Times*, no. 114 (March, 1988).

Bendau, C. P. (1979). *Colin Wilson: The Outsider and Beyond*. San Bernardino, CA: Borgo Press.

Bradfield, S. (1989). *Times Educational Supplement* (30 June 1989).

Burgess, A. (1988). Whips and petticoats. *The Observer* (21 February 1988).

Charlton, Professor B. (2015). http://charltonteaching.blogspot. co.uk/2015/01/cg-jung-psychopathic-genius.html (last accessed 11/2015)

Dossor, H. F. (1990). *Colin Wilson: The Man and his Mind*. Shaftesbury, Dorset: Element Books.

Fuller, P. (1988). In praise of older perverts. *The Guardian* (19 February 1988).

Greenwell, T. (1981). Shared experience. *The Yorkshire Post* (26 March 1981).

Heppenstall, J. R. (1959). A pious hope. *Times Literary Supplement* (4 September 1959).

King, M. (2010). Abundance now, harmony later. *Scientific and Medical Network Review*, no. 103 (Summer 2010): www.jnani.org/mrking/writings/ Post2010/Superconsciousness-full.html (last accessed 11/2015)

Kirkus Reviews. (November 1, 1988).

Lomas, H. (1972). Coffee table philosophy. *London Magazine* (August/ September 1972).

Loshak, D. (1981). Identity. *Now!* (20 February 1981).

Maltherne, B. (2004). www.doyletics.com/_arj1/lordofth.htm (last accessed 11/2015)

Maschler, T. (Ed.) (1957). *Declaration*. London: MacGibbon & Kee.

Maurer, R. (1963) More shooting stars from Colin Wilson. *New York Herald Tribune Books* (23 June 1963).

Moon, E. (1963). *Library Journal*, 88 (1 May 1963).

National Review. (1982). (25 June 1982).

Power, D. (2011). Colin Wilson's *Access to Inner Worlds*. In: C. Stanley (Ed.), *Around the Outsider: Essays Presented to Colin Wilson on the Occasion of His 80th Birthday*. Winchester: 0-Books.

Profumo, D. (1988). How to tumble your drier. *The Literary Review*, no. 117 (March, 1988).

Richardson, M. (1963). *New Statesman*, 65, (24 May 1963).

Rycroft, C. (1972). Still outside. *The Spectator* (27 May 1972).

Scott, D. (2014). www.goodreads.com/book/show/3423073-c-g-jung (last accessed 11/2015).

Stanley, C. (2015). *The Ultimate Colin Wilson Bibliography, 1956–2015*. Nottingham: Paupers' Press.

Storr, A. (1963). Ignorance and good intentions. *Sunday Times* (18 May 1963).

Storr, A. (1981). Reich: have box, will travel. *Sunday Times* (8 March 1981).

Sutherland, S. (1981). Brainstorm. *The Sunday Telegraph* (1 February 1981).

Walton, A. H. (1972). Freud and after. *Books & Bookmen* (July 1972).

Ward, G. (2009). The peak of perfection. *Western Daily Press Weekend Books* (28 March 2009).

Ward, G. (2011). Super consciousness: the quest for the peak experience. In: C. Stanley (Ed.), *Around the Outsider: Essays Presented to Colin Wilson on the Occasion of His 80th Birthday*. Winchester: 0-Books.

Weigel, J. A. (1975). *Colin Wilson*. Boston: G. K. Hall.

Wilson, C. (1963). Mr. Wilson writes a Siamese twin book. *The Yorkshire Post* (3 May 1963).

Wilson, C. (1966). *Sex and the Intelligent Teenager*. London: Arrow.

Wilson, C. (1970a). *Origins of the Sexual Impulse*. London: Panther Books (originally published: London: Arthur Barker, 1963).

Wilson, C. (1970b). *Poetry & Mysticism*. London: Hutchinson.

Wilson, C. (1972). *New Pathways in Psychology: Maslow and the post-Freudian revolution*. New York: Taplinger.

Wilson, C. (1973a). A doomed society? *Journal of Human Relations*, 21.

Wilson, C. (1973b). *The Occult*. St. Albans: Mayflower (originally published: London: Hodder & Stoughton, 1971).

Wilson, C. (1982). *The Quest for Wilhelm Reich*. St Albans: Granada (originally published by Granada in 1981).

Wilson, C. (1986a). *Access to Inner Worlds*. London: Rider (originally published by Rider in 1983).

Wilson, C. (1986b). *The Essential Colin Wilson* (CD). Wyastone Leys, Monmouth: Nimbus Records [NI 5124].

Wilson, C. (1988). *C. G. Jung: Lord of the Underworld*. Wellingborough, UK: Aquarian (first published by Aquarian in 1984 as *Lord of the Underworld: Jung and the Twentieth Century*).

Wilson, C. (1991). *Frankenstein's Castle: The Right Brain: Door to Wisdom*. Bath: Ashgrove Press (originally published by Ashgrove in 1980).

Wilson, C. (2001a). *The Age of Defeat*. Nottingham: Paupers' Press (originally published: London: Victor Gollancz, 1959).

Wilson, C. (2001b). The Moors murders. Introduction to: I. Brady, *The Gates of Janus: Serial Killing and its Analysis*. Los Angeles: Feral House.

Wilson, C. (2003). *Dreaming to Some Purpose*. London: Century.

Wilson, C. (2009). Afterword: Colin Wilson on "The Outsider Cycle". In: C. Stanley, *Colin Wilson's "Outsider Cycle": A Guide for Students*. Nottingham: Paupers' Press.

Wilson, C. (2009a). *Super Consciousness*. London: Watkins.

INDEX